Reference Books for Small and Medium-sized Public Libraries

Compiled by the
American Library Association
Reference Services Division
Basic Reference Books Committee

MARY C. BARTER, *Chairman*

American Library Association
Chicago 1969

Standard Book Number 8389–3092–1 (1969)

Library of Congress Catalog Card Number 68-24460

Copyright © 1969 by the American Library Association

Manufactured in the United States of America

Basic Reference Books Committee
Reference Services Division
American Library Association

LYNN H. ROBINSON
Principal Library Coordinator
Providence Public Library
Providence, R.I.
Formerly Reference
  Coordinator
Suffolk Cooperative Library
  System
Patchogue, N.Y.

IRENE ROGERS
Reference Librarian
Yonkers Public Library
Yonkers, N.Y.

ROBERT THOMAS
Principal Librarian in Charge
  of General Reference
Mid-Manhattan Library
New York Public Library
New York, N.Y.

(Mrs.) MARY C. BARTER
Chairman
Librarian, Springfield Town
  Library
Springfield, Vt.
Formerly Assistant Librarian
Central Library
Queens Borough Public Library
Jamaica, N.Y.

Preface

REFERENCE BOOKS FOR SMALL AND MEDIUM-SIZED PUBLIC LIBRARIES has been prepared to meet a long-standing and widespread need. It is designed to serve as an authoritative buying guide for the purchase of reference collections for newly established libraries and for improving and expanding existing collections. It is also intended to serve as a guide to be consulted by librarians when they must refer to larger library collections and make requests for interlibrary loan. The list provides bibliographic information and evaluative annotations for the most convenient and productive reference sources in all broad fields on levels usually encountered in public libraries.

Origin and History of List

Twice in recent years, the Reference Services Division has been faced with the necessity of doing crash programs of reference lists in connection with world fairs in Seattle and New York. Committees responsible for the crash lists performed highly commendable jobs, but the need remained for a published list based on more deliberate selection, with sufficient time for careful editing. Also, the Reference Services Division office at American Library Association headquarters is constantly asked by librarians throughout the country for a basic reference list. The Division's Board decided, therefore, at the Detroit Conference in 1965, to establish a Basic Reference Books Committee of the Division. By this action, the Board was seeking not only to avoid future crash programs in the preparation of reference lists, but also to create machinery to meet a fundamental responsibility of the Division—advisory service in the establishment of new reference collections and in the strengthening of existing ones. Members of the Committee, appointed in the fall of 1965, were librarians experienced in reference service, with knowledge of and access to extensive reference collections. All were within or close to the New York metropolitan area to facilitate working together.

Definition of Potential Users

The Committee defined small to medium-sized public libraries as those serving populations between 10,000 and 75,000. Libraries serving populations of less than 10,000 need to call on the other libraries of the area or their state library agency to give full reference service. Communities serving populations of more than 75,000 need stronger reference resources than this list suggests.

Through improved state aid programs and federally funded projects, library book budgets have increased steadily. More and more libraries are becoming part of county or multicounty systems with access to greatly augmented book collections. This list offers a selection which goes beyond a bare minimum of essential items, although many libraries cannot now afford all the titles included. As funds become available, as libraries prepare to expand their resources in one or more subject areas, and as inexperienced librarians seek to borrow material from regional or central libraries or to give referral service, this list can be a major source of consultation.

Scope

The list covers those adult reference books in print at time of compilation which would be generally useful in the small or medium-sized public library. The cut-off date of the list is December 31, 1966, but the Committee has included important works or new editions bearing 1967 or 1968 imprints if these appeared in time for examination and addition.

Reference books for children's collections are not within the scope of this list. Textbooks have been omitted also except where the text is the only work available to cover a particular subject. In selecting the items for inclusion and in judging the merits of the total list in each broad subject area, the Committee measured its work against an extensive group of earlier reference lists.

Many lists of reference books already exist. Some, such as *Guide to Reference Books,* edited by Constance M. Winchell, are too comprehensive for easy use in the smaller library. Others, such as *Suggested Reference Books for Small or Branch Public Libraries* (American Library Association Small Libraries Project), are too limited and lack descriptive annotations. Still others, such as the Enoch Pratt Free Library list, *Reference Books,* are aimed at the users of libraries and thus, although excellent tools, serve a different purpose. The annual *Library Journal List* offers good coverage of the new reference books each year, serving still another purpose.

The Committee has worked more than two years on this project. Realizing that any list is at least partially obsolete before it is published, it has made every possible effort to produce a practical and useful selection aid for librarians.

Format and Arrangement

The form of entry includes author, title, edition, publisher and date, paging (or volumes), price, and annotation. Names of publishers are given in abbreviated form. A directory of publishers' names and addresses is supplied on page 145. For serial publications, the initial date and frequency of publication are given. Although prices change constantly, they are included to give a general indication of the approximate cost of items.

The seventeen major subject categories follow the same sequence as the broad divisions of the Dewey Decimal Classification, with some modification to place related subjects together. Items included under each major subject are grouped by subtopic, form, or both. Classification numbers have been omitted because of variation in their use and the forced or illogical order that strict adherence to Dewey would have dictated. An author-subject-title index is provided.

Acknowledgments

The Chairman wishes to thank each committee member and all other librarians working in the several systems of the Greater New York area who contributed to this combined effort, with special thanks to Miss Julia Ruth Armstrong and Mrs. Elizabeth M. Quier, who worked as a subcommittee with the Chairman in the final preparation of the list. Mrs. Eleanore Meyer, of the Central Library office in Queens, typed the final draft of the list. Mrs. Emma Richardson efficiently handled the Committee's secretarial work. Thanks are due to the New York Public Library for the use of meeting rooms and to the Queens Borough Public Library for helpful cooperation in many ways. Librarians who use the list will be the best judges of its value.

MARY C. BARTER, *Chairman*
Basic Reference Books Committee

Contents

Reference Books for
Small and Medium-sized
Public Libraries

1
Books, Libraries, and the Book Trade

Bibliographical Sources

1 American book publishing record. Bowker, 1960– . Monthly. $15.50 a year.

A monthly periodical that accumulates by subject, according to the Dewey Decimal Classification system, all books listed in the Weekly Record section of *Publishers' Weekly*. Entries give price, classification number, Library of Congress subject heading, catalog card number, publisher, and a brief description of the book. Contains indexes by author and by title. There are cumulations with same arrangement and scope: 1960–64, 3v., $79.95; 1965, 1433p., $25; 1966, 1606p., $25.

2 Books in print: an author-title-series index to the Publishers' trade list annual. Bowker, 1948– . Annually in Oct. 2v.: Authors; Titles. $19.85.

Lists all books in print. Author index volume gives date, price, and publisher. Title index volume gives only price and publisher; a directory of publishers is included.

3 Subject guide to Books in print: a subject index to the Publishers' trade list annual. Bowker, 1957– . Annually in Oct. $18.25.

The *Subject Guide* arranges the books listed in *Books in Print* by Library of Congress subject headings with many cross references. Full bibliographic information is given. Omitted are fiction, poetry, drama, juvenile fiction, Bibles, and books priced at less than 25 cents.

4 Forthcoming books. Bowker, 1966–   . Bimonthly. $12 a year.
   A supplement to *Books in Print* which provides separate author and title indexes to books which are to appear in the next five-month period. Gives prices, publisher, and expected publication date.

5 Subject guide to forthcoming books. Bowker, 1967–   . Bimonthly. $7.50 a year. Special combination rate for subscriptions to both Forthcoming Books and Subject Guide, $18 a year.
   This provides a subject volume for *Forthcoming Books* in 160 different subject areas.

6 Cumulative book index; a world list of books in the English language. Wilson, 1898–   . Monthly except Aug. Service basis.
   Scope was widened in 1928 to include books and pamphlets in English issued in the United States and Canada, and a selection of publications from other parts of the English-speaking world. Dictionary arrangement. Does not include government documents or pamphlets. For plan of cumulation, consult the catalog of *Wilson Publications*.

7 Orton, Robert Merritt, ed. Catalog of reprints in series. 20th ed. Scarecrow, 1965. 982p. $25. Supplement, 1967. 285p. $8.
   Useful for checking the various editions of books available in the many series issued by publishers. Part 1 is a dictionary catalog of author and title entries. Full bibliographic information is given in each main entry. Part 2 is an alphabetical list of publishers and series.

8 Paperbound books in print. Bowker, 1955–   . Monthly. $16 a year.
   A monthly listing of paperbacks available with a three-times-a-year (Oct., Feb., June) cumulative index. Arranged by author, by title, and by subject. Also includes previews of the month ahead.

9 Publishers' trade list annual. Bowker, 1873– . Annually in fall (1966 issue has 4v.). $14.

A compilation of the actual catalogs of more than 1600 publishers. Amount of information supplied by publishers varies. Volume 1 contains index of publishers, followed by catalogs of small publishing houses. Bulk of set consists of catalogs arranged alphabetically by publishers.

10 Publishers' weekly; the book industry journal. Bowker, 1872– . Weekly. $15 a year.

Provides news of the book trade. Its great value to librarians is the weekly listing of new books as they are being published. Full bibliographic information is given for each title. Spring, Summer, and Fall issues of books to come are also useful.

Book Lists and Selection Aids

11 The Booklist and Subscription books bulletin. American Library Assn. Sept. 1956– . Semimonthly Sept.–July; monthly in Aug. $10 a year. (Formerly The Booklist, 1905–56, and Subscription books bulletin, 1930–56.)

The Booklist is a book-selection tool, buying guide, and cataloging aid devoted to impartial, factual appraisals of new books recommended for library purchase. Separate sections for adult, young adult, and children's books. Descriptive, critical notes for each title summarize content and point out special uses or features. Complete ordering and cataloging information is given for each title. In the Subscription Books Bulletin section are detailed, objective evaluations of reference books and sets—clearly recommended or not recommended—by ALA's Subscription Books Committee. Special sections and lists appear on films, government publications, pamphlets, paperbacks, and bibliographies in fields of current interest. Subject-author-title index in each issue; semiannual and annual cumulative indexes.

12 Committee on College Reading. Good reading. New Amer. Lib., 1964. 287p. Paper $.75.

Since its first appearance in 1933, this guide to serious reading in 28 subject fields has been frequently revised. In this issue there are about 2000 titles, selected and annotated by the Committee on College Reading, sponsored by the College English Association. Contains a list of 100 significant books and 100 major reference titles. Indexed.

13 Hoffman, Hester R. J., ed. Reader's adviser; an annotated guide to the best in print in literature, biographies, dictionaries, encyclopedias, Bibles, classics, drama, poetry, fiction, science, philosophy, travel, history. 10th ed., rev. and enl. Bowker, 1964. 1292p. $20. (New ed. in prep.)

Designed primarily to help booksellers and librarians in choosing editions but good for the general reader, who will find its annotations useful. Although not so current as the *Subject Guide to Books in Print,* it is more helpful because it is selective, whereas the *Subject Guide,* by its very nature, is not.

14 Subscription books bulletin reviews. American Library Assn. 1961–   . Volumes for 1956–60; 1960–62; 1962–64; 1964–66. Paper $2.25; $1.50; $2; $2.25.

Compilation of reference book reviews which appeared in *The Booklist and Subscription Books Bulletin* for the years indicated. 1964–66 volume has a cumulative index for the years 1956–66.

15 Wilson, H. W., *firm, publishers.* Fiction catalog. 7th ed. Wilson, 1960. 650p. $9.

Differs from earlier editions in form. Part 1 is an author list of 4097 works of fiction with full bibliographical information; annotations for each book are designed to show its nature. Part 2 is a title and subject index to Part 1 and also contains a directory of publishers.

————1961–65 volume. 1966. 299p. $11. (Price includes the four annual supplements noted below.)

————Four annual supplements, 1967–70.

Primarily a selection aid, but also useful for readers' advisory service.

16 Winchell, Constance M. Guide to reference books. 8th ed. American Library Assn., 1967. 741p. $15. 1st supplement, 1965–1966. Edited by Eugene P. Sheehy, 1968. 122p. $3.50.

This new edition of an important reference tool and selection aid lists about 7500 reference books basic to research and serves as a manual for the library assistant and research worker.

Indexes to Materials

► Indexes of periodicals and/or books and pamphlets are essential for reference use, as well as for book selection and ordering. They are important in a reference collection for the identification of material, although this material may not be owned by the library. They can be used to facilitate interlibrary loans from larger collections. They also provide desiderata for strengthening the library's own resources. Indexes of material in a particular subject field will be found under the subject.

17 Book review digest . . . Wilson, 1905– . Monthly except Feb. and July, with annual cumulation. Service basis.

An index to current reviews in approximately 75 English and American periodicals, with excerpts and digests. Each issue has a title and subject index. Issues for 1905–59 are available at prices ranging from $5 to $15 per volume.

18 Book review index. Gale Res., 1965– . Monthly with cumulations. $24 a year.

Differs from *Book Review Digest* in that it is solely an author index with only review sources cited. Indexes all reviews in approximately 200 sources.

19 Guide to microforms in print. Microcard Editions, Inc., 1961– . Annual. $4.

An alphabetically arranged guide to materials of United States publishers available on microfilm or other microforms. Does not list theses and dissertations. Essentially a price list.

20 Subject guide to Microforms in print, 1962/63–   . Microcard Editions, Inc., 1962–   . Annual. $4.

Lists, under subject classifications, the material listed in *Guide to Microforms in Print.*

21 New York Times index. New York Times Co., 1913–   . Semimonthly, $75 a year; annual cumulation, $75; combined service $125.

Useful in locating articles not only in the *New York Times* but in other papers as well, since entries establish the date of an occurrence. Indexes for earlier years of the *Times* may be obtained from publisher: 1851–1912, 12v. $44.50 each.

22 Public Affairs Information Service. Bulletin. The Service. 1915–   . Weekly; cumulated five times a year. Weekly and cumulated bulletins and annual volume, $100; cumulated bulletins and annual volume, $50; annual cumulation, $25.

A subject index to periodicals, pamphlets, and government documents relating to the social sciences, public administration, and related topics.

23 Readers' guide to periodical literature. Wilson, 1900–   . Semimonthly, Sept.–June; monthly July and Aug., with quarterly and permanent, bound annual cumulations. $28 a year.

An author-title-subject index to about 158 general and non-technical magazines. Essential in any library. Volumes 1–27 (1900–1968) in print at $28 per volume.

24 Union list of serials in the United States and Canada. 3d ed. Wilson, 1965. 5v. $120.

A guide to the location of periodical files and the availability of copies either through interlibrary loan or photocopy in 956 American and Canadian libraries. This edition covers 156,499 serial titles in existence through December, 1949.

25 U.S. Library of Congress. New serial titles, 1950–1960; a

supplement to the Union list of serials. 3d ed. Library of Congress, 1961, 1966. 2v. $56.25 the set. Continued by monthly issues and annual cumulations. $95 a year.

Besides locating periodicals in a number of libraries, gives information on name changes, mergers, and cessation of periodicals. A three-volume cumulation for 1961–65 is available from Bowker ($38.35).

26 Vertical file index. Wilson, 1935– . Monthly except Aug. $8 a year.

A list of selected pamphlets of interest for the general library. These are current and available. Arrangement is by subject, with title, publisher, date, paging, and price. A descriptive note is usually given. Contains an index by title.

Directories

27 American book trade directory. Edited by Eleanor F. Steiner-Prag. Bowker, 1915– . Biennial. $25.

Includes lists of publishers in the United States, former publishing companies, dealers in foreign books, exporters, importers, and wholesalers, and an international directory of booksellers. Bookstores are arranged under state and city with speciality of each noted.

28 American library directory; a classified list of libraries, with names of librarians and statistical data. Bowker, 1923– . Biennial. $25.

Includes United States and Canadian public, college, and special libraries arranged by state, city, and institution. Subject strengths are indicated.

29 Ayer, *firm, newspaper advertising agents.* N. W. Ayer and Son's Directory of newspapers and periodicals. Ayer, 1880– . Annual. $30.

Geographical list of periodical publications in the United

States, Canada, Bermuda, the Republic of Panama, and the Republic of the Philippines. Size, format, periodicity, and political sympathies are indicated. Also includes economic, statistical, and climatic information for each state and city. Classified lists include agricultural, collegiate, foreign language, Negro, religious, fraternal, trade and technical, labor, etc., publications. Indexed.

30 Literary market place, the business directory of American book publishing. Bowker, 1940– . Annual. Paper $7.45.

Useful for a variety of publishing data. Includes information on publishers, book manufacturers, book reviewers, literary agents, literary awards and fellowships, and periodical agencies. Helpful to amateur writer in selecting a publisher.

31 Standard periodical directory. 2d ed. Oxbridge Pub. Co., 1967. 1019p. $25.

A subject listing of more than 30,000 United States and Canadian periodicals, often with brief annotations. Title index.

32 Ulrich's International periodicals directory. Bowker. v.I. 12th ed. 1967. Scientific, medical, technical periodicals; v.II. 12th ed. 1968. Arts, humanities, social sciences, and business magazines. $15 each volume.

Classified and selected list of current foreign and domestic periodicals. Complete publishing and subscription information given. Especially helpful is notation of indexing and abstracting services in which each periodical is indexed and abstracted. Supplement issued annually in early fall to update both volumes ($6.95).

Miscellaneous

33 Baer, Eleanora A. Titles in series: a handbook for librarians and students. 2d ed. Scarecrow, 1964. 2v. $42.50. Supplement, 1967. 391p. $10.

Volume 1 lists titles of books in many series. Volume 2 contains an author and title index to individual titles, an index to series titles, and a directory of publishers. Useful tool for catalogers, reference, and acquisition librarians.

34 Leidy, W. P. A popular guide to government publications. 3d ed. Columbia Univ. Pr., 1968. 365p. $12.

More than 100 subject lists of inexpensive, authoritative, in-print materials from Adolescence to World War II. Price of each item given.

35 U.S. Government Printing Office. Price lists. Govt. Print. Off., 1898–   . (Various subjects) Single copies free.

Each price list provides a useful guide to inexpensive and up-to-date materials published by the federal government.

36 U.S. Library of Congress. Processing Dept. Monthly checklist of state publications. Govt. Print. Off., 1910–   . $3 per year (including annual index).

Lists official publications of the various states. (State libraries and state library associations frequently publish bibliographies for their own states.)

37 U.S. Superintendent of Documents. Monthly catalog of government publications. Govt. Print. Off., 1895–   . Annual subscription $4.50.

More extensive guide to United States publications than the *Price Lists*. Each issue has a subject index which is cumulated in December.

38 Wilson, H. W., *firm, publishers*. Standard catalog for public libraries; a classified & annotated list of 7,610 non-fiction books recommended for public & college libraries, with a full author, title, subject, and analytical index. Compiled by Dorothy Herbert West and Estelle A. Fidell. 4th ed. Wilson, 1958. 1349p. $30.

————1959–1963. 1964. 526p. $25. (Price includes four annual supplements.)

————Four annual supplements, 1967–70.

Selected titles in all fields with full cataloging information.

39 Writer's market. Writer's Digest. Annual. $7.95.

Information on agents and markets for free-lance artists, photographers, and authors. A subject listing of special-interest markets from Astrology to Women's Magazines. Each listing includes name and address of the publication or company, its editorial needs, and its rate of payment. Additional lists of syndicates, writers' conferences, and writers' clubs are useful for amateur author.

2
Encyclopedias

► Each library reference collection will need one or more encyclopedias, depending upon its public and upon the purchases and location of the Children's Room, if there is a separate room for this age group. It is advisable in a larger reference collection to buy consistently the annuals for the encyclopedias purchased. In some smaller collections, this may not be necessary. If several encyclopedias are purchased, buy sets at staggered intervals, so that there will always be a recent one.

In the following list, annotations are descriptive. There is no attempt to indicate priority among the multivolume sets, but the following title may be used as a guide to the evaluation of encyclopedias:

40 Walsh, S. Padraig, comp. General encyclopedias in print: a comparative analysis. Bowker. Annual. $3.

This small handbook will help a prospective buyer evaluate an encyclopedia, as it describes in detail the arrangement, age suitability, history, subject coverage, reviews, and many other items of information about the principal encyclopedias published. Consensus of opinion rating chart (by professional librarians and educators) lists encyclopedias in three groups: recommended, not-recommended, and discontinued.

41 Collier's Encyclopedia. Collier-Macmillan Library Service. 24v. $329.50.

An adult encyclopedia, suitable for junior and senior high school students as well as for college and university students. Articles are well developed, well presented, and well illustrated. Arrangement is alphabetical, letter by letter. The scholarly, signed articles vary in length according to importance of subject treated. The set is especially useful for its coverage of politics, biography, fine arts, religion, philosophy, the classics, science, and technology. Small topical maps and large (many multicolored) maps with adjacent gazetteer information accompany articles on states, provinces, and countries. The list of contributors appears in Volume 1 and notes the qualifications and writings of each specialist. Volume 24 contains the bibliography; a comprehensive, analytical index; and a study guide designed to aid the reader seeking to enlarge his knowledge on a particular subject. Bibliographies are listed under broad subject fields, explicitly subdivided, with title entries arranged under broad or narrow subjects according to the scope of the books listed; generally the books begin at high school level and progress through college and postcollege levels, with easier or general works treated first. Continuous revision program, with several printings a year, assures up-to-dateness.

42 Collier's Yearbook. $4.95.

Supplement and annual survey.

43 Compton's Pictured encyclopedia and fact-index. Encyclopaedia Britannica. 15v. $134. plus delivery charge.

A juvenile encyclopedia for home and school use. Designed to meet requirements of school curricula and interests of children from grade 4 through high school. Can be used by parents and teachers who wish to help children help themselves, and contains articles on important phases of family life written for adults. Arrangement is letter by letter, and each volume, consisting of one or more complete letters of the alphabet, is divided into two parts. The main text (Part I) is an alphabetical arrangement of principal articles on broad subjects. These are well illustrated with pictures, charts, and diagrams, and contain cross references. Articles on states include a fact summary and maps with gazetteer information. Coverage on scientific subjects is good. Some of the main text articles contain reference-outlines which refer to other articles in the set, and bibliographies which refer to significant books in print; the bibliographies for major articles are divided into two lists, one for younger readers and the other for advanced students and teachers. Part II is a Fact-Index which incorporates dictionary type of information and brief biographical sketches with an analytical index of all text and illustrative material in that particular volume. Articles are not signed, but the speciality of each contributor is noted in the list of consultants and contributors in Volume 1. Maintains a continuous revision program with several printings a year.

44 Compton's Yearbook. $7.95.
    Supplement and annual record.

45 Encyclopedia Americana. Grolier. 30v. $299.50.
    A popular adult encyclopedia which is also suitable for junior and senior high school as well as college and university students. Arrangement is alphabetical, word by word. Articles are well developed and presented in a style easy to understand. For the most part the articles are short, but articles on subjects of major importance are lengthy and are signed by the specialist who wrote them. Articles are well illustrated. Bibliographies appear at the end of major articles and list authoritative sources for further information; for longer articles, bibliographies are subdivided into topics relating to sections of the article. Large multicolored maps with gazetteer information and smaller topical maps accompany text on states and countries. The last volume contains an illustrated section of chronological world events for the preceding five years and a comprehensive, ana-

lytical index which may be used as a study guide. Continuous revision with several printings a year. Valuable for its articles on science, technology, biography, topics of American interests, and digests of opera, drama, and books. The list of contributors in Volume 2 indicates specific articles each contributor has written for the set.

46 Americana annual. $12.
   Supplement and annual survey.

47 Encyclopaedia Britannica. Encyclopaedia Britannica. 24v. $299.

The most famous, scholarly, and oldest English-language adult encyclopedia still in existence; suitable for high school, college, and university students, and mature adults. Arrangement is alphabetical, letter by letter, in broad subject articles with many subheads and in shorter articles on specific topics. Lengthy articles are prefaced with a table of contents, have cross references, and include excellent bibliographies of works in English and some in foreign languages. The articles are signed with the initials of the contributing specialist, who is identified and whose qualifications are noted in the Index volume. The Index is comprehensive and definitive, making any specific information in the set easily and exactly located. The Index volume also contains a world atlas of over 200 multicolored maps and an atlas index. Well illustrated. Maintains systematic and continuous revision, and updating of important subjects for each annual printing. Especially noted for coverage on civics, literature, science, art, geography, biography, and history.

48 Britannica book of the year. $8.95.
   Supplement and annual survey.

49 World book encyclopedia. Field Enterprises. 20v. $179.80.

A good encyclopedia for young people from elementary grades through high school, and popular also as a general adult encyclopedia. Articles are written at the school level for which specific subjects are likely to be studied. Arrangement is alphabetical, word by word. Articles are clear, concise and factual, the length depending on the importance of the subject treated, and they are signed. The list of contributors in Volume 1 gives the title of articles each specialist has contributed to the set. Well-illustrated, multicolored maps have their own index on adjacent pages. While there is no index to the set, there are copious cross references. Major articles contain study aids: lists of related articles, frequently an outline, pertinent questions for understanding comprehension, and separate lists of books for further reading for young readers, and for older readers. Especially useful for scientific subjects, literature, art, and biography. Maintains a continuous revision program.

50 World book year book, an annual supplement. $5.95.

Encyclopedias (One Volume)

51 Columbia encyclopedia. Edited by William Bridgwater and Seymour Kurtz. 3d ed. Columbia Univ. Pr., 1963. 2388p. $49.50.

A one-volume encyclopedia with entries arranged in alphabetical order. An excellent source for quick identification at the library information desk. Treatment of subjects is brief.

52 Lincoln library of essential information. Frontier Pr., 1966. 2v. ed. $47.50 and $52.50; 1v. ed. $42.50.

Information in this reference book is arranged by subject under rather broad headings. The arrangement emphasizes self-education, but the addition of a full index makes it a convenient source of factual information.

3
Philosophy and Religion

Bibliographies

53 Adams, Charles J., ed. A reader's guide to the great religions. Free Pr., 1965. 364p. $9.95.

Bibliographic essays on the major religious traditions of mankind. Contributors are specialists, but the audience is the general reader. Title selection is based on availability and readability, with emphasis on English-language publications. Reference works and periodicals are also listed. Indexed by author (translator, editor, etc.) and by subject.

54 Diehl, Katharine Smith. Religions, mythologies, folklores; an annotated bibliography. 2d ed. Scarecrow, 1962. 573p. $12.50.

Useful bibliography of materials published 1900–1960 on literature of faith and practice in all cultures for layman, scholar, and librarian. Arranged by broad subject, and includes brief annotations. Indexed.

Dictionaries, Encyclopedias, and Handbooks

55 Catholic dictionary (The Catholic encyclopaedic dictionary). Edited by Donald Attwater. 3d ed. Macmillan, 1958. 552p. $6.50; paper $2.45.

Contains brief but complete definitions of religious terms and associations, including histories of the latter when necessary. Ecclesiastical calendar of the Church, and titles and modes of address are also given.

56 Encyclopedia of philosophy. Paul Edwards, editor in chief. Macmillan, 1967. 8v. $219.50.

Scholarly work, but within the understanding of the general reader. Covers, for all periods, both Oriental and Western philosophers, concepts, and schools of philosophy. Useful also for investigating peripheral fields in the sciences and social sciences. Signed articles; contributors represent subject authority on international level. Good bibliographies follow articles. Full cross referencing is sometimes lacking, but there is a good index. Major contribution to a field where a new encyclopedic work has long been needed.

57 Gibb, H. A. R., and Kramers, J. H., eds. Shorter encyclopaedia of Islam. Cornell Univ. Pr., 1953. 671p. $20.
Covers people, customs, places, and beliefs relating to the Islamic religion and law. Where needed, the history of a place or event is given. Bibliographies.

58 Jewish encyclopedia; a descriptive record of the history, religion, literature, and customs of the Jewish people from the earliest times to the present day. Prepared . . . under the direction of Cyrus Adler (and others) . . . Isidore Singer, managing ed. . . . Ktav, 1964. 12v. $69.50.
Basic information about the Jewish people, their customs and beliefs. Dated, but still useful for its historical and biographical coverage. Reprint of the 1901–6 edition.

59 Julian, John. A dictionary of hymnology, setting forth the origin and history of Christian hymns of all ages and nations. 2d rev. ed. Dover, 1957. 2v. $17.50.
Main entry is by title, with author and first-line indexes. Provides histories of hymns and their location in hymnals. Articles on hymnody and biographies of writers and translators included. English-language hymns emphasized. Reprint of the edition published originally in 1907.

60 Magill, Frank N., ed. Masterpieces of world philosophy in summary form. Harper, 1961. 1166p. $9.95; lib. bdg. $8.97.
Synopses of basic philosophical works from ancient to modern times. Includes a glossary of philosophical terms.

61 Mead, Frank S. Handbook of denominations in the United States. 4th ed. Abingdon, 1965. 271p. $2.95.
Handbook arranged by denomination, giving the history and

basic beliefs of each. Glossary, bibliography, and index. Gives church membership in United States by religious bodies.

62 New Catholic encyclopedia . . . Prepared by an editorial staff at the Catholic University of America . . . McGraw-Hill, 1967. 15v. $550. ($450 to libraries)

A major new tool which is not a revision of, but largely replaces, the Gilmary Society publication now out of print:

63 Catholic encyclopedia. . . . Edited by Charles G. Herbermann (*et al.*). Gilmary Society, 1907–22, 1950-54. 18v. (includes 2 suppls.)

The old *Catholic Encyclopedia* (cited above) is now mainly of historical interest, reflecting Church thinking earlier in the century. In those communities where need dictates and space allows, retention of the old set may be advisable. The *New Catholic Encyclopedia* is highly objective, modern, and ecumenical in tone. Retains a high level of scholarship, yet is generally more readable than the old. Many contributors are non-Catholic.

64 Oxford dictionary of the Christian Church. Edited by F. L. Cross. Oxford Univ. Pr., 1957. 1492p. $20.

Scholarly and useful dictionary for terms and names associated with the Christian faith. Old Testament names are also included. Bibliographies at end of most articles.

65 Schaff-Herzog encyclopedia. Twentieth century encyclopedia of religious knowledge; an extension of the New Schaff-Herzog encyclopedia of religious knowledge. Editor in chief, Lefferts A. Loetscher. Baker Book House, 1955. 2v. $15.

Description of religious affairs and personalities of the first half of the twentieth century. Concise, signed articles, many with bibliography. Although a supplement to the *New Schaff-Herzog Encyclopedia,* this can be used independently.

66 Urmson, James O., ed. Concise encyclopedia of Western philosophy and philosophers. Hawthorn, 1960. 431p. $15.

Short articles defining philosophical terms, descriptions of well-known "isms," accounts of individual philosophers, and general descriptions of main fields of philosophical inquiry for the beginning student. Includes illustrations, portraits, and bibliographies.

67 Zaehner, Robert Charles, ed. Concise encyclopedia of living faiths. Beacon, 1959. 431p. $3.95.

Gives the history of the major religions of the world today, with a chapter devoted to each. Index and bibliography.

Yearbooks

68 American Jewish year book. Jewish Pub. 1899–   . $6.50.

International in scope. Covers all aspects of Jewish activities, and includes population statistics and directories of organizations, Jewish periodicals, necrology, American Jewish bibliography, and Jewish calendar.

69 National Catholic almanac. Doubleday, 1904–   . $3.95.

Basic current information about the Catholic church and its members. Includes such dividends as a list of Catholic periodicals, books, writers' market, theater, radio and TV programs, and awards.

70 Official Catholic directory. Kenedy, 1886–   . $15.

For each diocese, lists churches, schools, hospitals, clergy, and religious orders. Also gives statistical information, places in the United States having resident pastor, alphabetical list of clergy, Eastern rites, and necrology.

71 Yearbook of American churches: information on all faiths in the U.S.A. Edited by Benson Y. Landis. National Council of the Churches of Christ in the U.S.A. 1916–   . $7.50.

Directory and statistical information on many religious organizations and service agencies; accredited seminaries, colleges, and universities; and religious periodicals.

Bibles

▶ Protestant, Roman Catholic, and Jewish versions of the Bible should be in every reference collection. The following title is useful in selecting an edition or printing:

72 Hester, Goldia, comp. and ed. Guide to Bibles in print. Richard Gordon and Associates, 1966. Paper $3.
   Lists various editions of Bibles in print, treating the Old and New Testaments separately. Indicates size, price, type of binding, and other pertinent information. Includes a list of available foreign language scriptures and a selected list of Bible reference books. The discussion of Bibles in *The Reader's Adviser,* edited by Hester Hoffman (see no. 13), is useful for selecting desirable versions.

Dictionaries and Encyclopedias

73 Hastings, James, ed. Dictionary of the Bible. Rev. ed. by Frederick C. Grant and H. H. Rowley. Scribner, 1963. 1059p. $15.
   Identification of people and places found in the Bible, as well as explanation of biblical terms. Based on Revised Standard Version. Hastings is a work of long standing; this revision, based on recent research, brings the 1930 edition up to date. Contains 10 pages of maps.

74 McKenzie, John L. Dictionary of the Bible. Bruce, 1965. 954p. $17.95; paper $5.95.
   Highly authoritative treatment by a Catholic scholar. Balanced, objective, ecumenical, and based on solid archaeological research. Contains an up-to-date, although brief, bibliography. Good illustrations and maps. Complements Hastings, but is more appropriate for the nonscholar.

75 Miller, Madeleine S., and Miller, J. Lane. Encyclopedia of Bible life. Rev. ed. Harper, 1955. 493p. $8.95.
   A dependable contribution to visual biblical education for teachers, ministers, and students. Arranged in broad topics—

such as Agriculture, Arts and Crafts, Business Transactions, Defense, etc.—with bibliography for each chapter. Well illustrated and indexed.

76 Harper's Bible dictionary. 7th ed. Harper, 1962. 854p. $8.95.
Not so comprehensive as Hastings or McKenzie, but has satisfactory treatment of biblical people, places, and things.

Concordances and Quotation Books

► There are several concordances corresponding to each of the various versions of the Bible. In the following selection, the title or the note indicates that version of the Bible on which each concordance is based.

77 Cruden, Alexander. Cruden's Unabridged concordance to the Old and New Testaments and the Apocrypha. Baker Book House, 1953. 719p. $5.95.
King James Version. The special value of this work is that Cruden provides an index to the Apocrypha. Note that some reprints of the work omit the Apocrypha concordance.

78 Ellison, John W., ed. Nelson's Complete concordance of the Revised Standard Version Bible. Nelson, 1957. 2157p. $15.
The most complete concordance of this version. Computer-produced.

79 Joy, Charles R. Harper's Topical concordance. Rev. and enl. ed. Harper, 1962. 628p. $8.95.
King James Version. A subject, rather than a word, concordance. One can, for example, check under such contemporary concepts as "integration" to find pertinent Bible passages.

80 Stevenson, Burton E. Home book of Bible quotations. Harper, 1949. 645p. $10.
Quotations from the King James Version of the Bible, including Apocrypha, are arranged by subject. Includes a word concordance with citation to book, chapter, and verse in the Bible.

81 Strong, James. Exhaustive concordance of the Bible . . . Abingdon, 1958. 1340, 262, 126, 79p. (4v. in 1) $15.75.

Main part of the book contains most complete concordance to the Bible. Other parts: comparative concordance of the authorized and revised versions of the text of the canonical books of the Holy Scriptures, concise dictionary of the words in the Hebrew Bible with their renderings in the Authorized English Version, and a Greek dictionary of the New Testament.

82 Thompson, Newton W., and Stock, Raymond. Complete concordance to the Bible (Douay Version). 4th rev. and enl. ed. Herder, 1945. 1914p. $17.

Needed for location of texts in the Douay Bible.

Atlases

83 May, Herbert G., and others, ed. Oxford Bible atlas. Oxford Univ. Pr., 1962. 144p. $4.95; paper $2.50.

Includes physical, historical, and archaeological maps. Text gives history, including dates of rulers. Gazetteer lists names on maps with Bible references wherever applicable.

84 Wright, George Ernest, and Filson, Floyd Vivian. Westminster historical atlas to the Bible. Rev. ed. Westminster, 1956. 130p. $7.50.

In addition to maps, contains text, illustrations, and chronological outlines of ancient history. Revision takes into account the discovery of the Dead Sea Scrolls. Besides a good general index there is an index to modern place-names and a tabulation of biblical sites. Places named in the Bible can be readily located. Also includes index of Arabic names identified with biblical places in Syria and Palestine.

Other Sacred Writings

► The sacred writings of religions other than Jewish and Christian may be needed. For example:

85 Koran. Trans. by J. M. Rodwell. Dutton [n.d.]. (Everyman's edition) 506p. $2.25.

86 Warren, Henry Clark, ed. and tr. Buddhism in translations; passages selected from the Buddhist sacred books and translated from the original Pāli into English. Atheneum, 1963. 496p. Paper $1.95.

Mythology and Folklore

Indexes and Bibliographies

87 Eastman, Mary Huse. Index to fairy tales, myths, and legends. 2d ed. rev. and enl. Faxon, 1926. 610p. $8.
————Supplement, 1937. 566p. $8.
————2d supplement, 1952. 370p. $8.
    Although this is an essential reference book for the Children's Department, it is a valuable source for the location of much folklore and fairy-tale material and should be available in adult book collections.

88 Haywood, Charles. A bibliography of North American folklore and folksong. 2d rev. ed. Dover, 1961. 2v. $15 the set. Peter Smith. $12.50.
    Contents: v.1, General works; regional studies; ethnic and occupational bibliographies; v.2, Folklore, music, ethnology, literature of North American Indians and Eskimos. Covers folklore bibliography in books, periodicals, monographs, recordings, and music publications. Index of composers, arrangers, and performers. General index. This edition is a corrected reprint of the 1951 edition.

Dictionaries and Encyclopedias

89 Frazer, *Sir* James G. New Golden bough; a new abridgement of the classic work. Edited . . . by Theodor H. Gaster. S. G. Phillips, 1959. 738p. $10; paper $1.25 (New Amer. Lib.); paper $2.45 (Doubleday).
    Excellent interpretation of the evolution of beliefs and customs related to magic and religion. Satisfactory substitute for

Frazer's original multivolume work, still available from St. Martin's Press at $125 the set.

90 Funk and Wagnalls Standard dictionary of folklore, mythology and legend. Maria Leach, ed.; Jerome Fried, associate ed. Funk, 1949–50. 2v. $10 each.

Many aspects of folklore are included in this work. Contributors include anthropologists and sociologists, so that the emphasis is on the ethnic rather than the literary side.

91 Robbins, Rossell Hope. Encyclopedia of witchcraft and demonology. Crown, 1959. 571p. $7.50.

Facts, history, and legend from medieval times (1450) to 1750. Extensive bibliography. Illustrations.

92 Sykes, Egerton, comp. Everyman's dictionary of non-classical mythology. Rev. ed. Dutton, 1961. 280p. $4.25.

Characters, legends, deities, and place-names from mythology outside the classical world are listed in one alphabet. Geographical coverage includes Europe, Asia, Middle East, Africa, the Pacific, and North and South America.

Handbooks

93 Botkin, Benjamin Albert, ed. A treasury of American folklore. Crown, 1944. 932p. $5.95.

Legends of the backwoods, badmen, heroes and demigods, boosters and knockers, humorous anecdotes and jests, tall tales and yarns, ballads and songs, are included in this collection. Index of authors, titles, and first lines of songs; index of subjects and names.

94 Bulfinch, Thomas. Bulfinch's Mythology: The age of fable; The age of chivalry; Legends of Charlemagne. Rev. ed. Crowell, 1962. 957p. $5.95.

Legends and myths from Greek, Roman, and Eastern mythologies. Stories of King Arthur and Charlemagne are also included. Dictionary-index.

95 Gayley, Charles M. Classic myths in English literature and
in art. Rev. ed. Blaisdell Pub., 1939. 597p. $6.95.
   Although not revised since 1939, Gayley is still an excellent
source for the explanation of Greek, Roman, Norse, and German myths.

96 Norton, Daniel S., and Rushton, Peters. Classical myths in
English literature. Holt, 1952. 444p. $6.75.
   Characters and events from Greek and Roman myths, alphabetically arranged, with illustrations of their use in classical and
in English and American literatures. Literary references are
indexed.

4
Psychology

Bibliographies

97 Harvard University. Harvard list of books in psychology. 3d
ed. Harvard Univ. Pr., 1964. 111p. Paper $2.50.
   An extensive bibliography, useful as a buying guide. Grouped
by type of psychology—such as Physiological, Comparative
animal, Personality, Social, etc. Brief annotations for each title.

Dictionaries and Handbooks

98 Baldwin, James M., ed. Dictionary of philosophy and psychology. Peter Smith, [n.d.]. 3v. v.1, $15; v.2, $15; v.3 in 2 pts.,
$10 each.
   Reprint of 1925 edition; old but still valid. Volumes 1 and 2
comprise the *Dictionary of Philosophical and Psychological
Terms* and include brief biographical information about philosophers, theologists, and persons whose lives may be of interest
to psychologists. Volume 3 is Benjamin Rand's *Bibliography of
Philosophy.* Illustrations, plates, and diagrams.

99 English, Horace B., and English, Ava C. A comprehensive
dictionary of psychological and psychoanalytical terms: a guide
to usage. McKay, 1958. 594p. $10.75.
   Most up-to-date one-volume dictionary of psychological and
psychoanalytical terms. Pronunciations are given.

100 Woodworth, Robert S., and Sheehan, Mary R. Contemporary
schools of psychology. 3d ed. Ronald, 1964. 457p. $6.50.
   Standard textbook in the field, providing excellent material
about each school of psychology. Indexed.

5
Business and Economics

Bibliographies

101 Coman, Edwin. Sources of business information. 2d ed. Univ.
of California Pr., 1964. 330p. $8.50.
   Could be called a guide to the literature of business, and is
a standard in its field. Arranged under subject divisions. Many
of the titles are annotated. Indexed.

102 Johnson, H. Webster, and McFarland, Stuart S. How to
use the business library. 3d ed. South-Western, 1964. 160p.
Paper $2.
   A basic, inexpensive guide to the use of any business library,
as well as a fine extensive listing of the important books in
the field. Sections on government publication and trade and
commercial organizations are very good. Well annotated and
indexed.

Indexes

103 Business periodicals index. Wilson, 1958–   . Monthly except
July, with annual cumulation. Service basis.
   A subject index to periodicals in the fields of accounting,

advertising, automation, banking, communications, economics, finance and investments, insurance, labor, management, marketing, taxes, etc. When the *Industrial Arts Index* was divided into two separate indexes in 1958, *Business Periodicals Index* and *Applied Science and Technology Index* were established.

General Works

104 Barach, Arnold B. U.S.A. and its economic future. Macmillan, 1964. 148p. $1.95.

A Twentieth Century Fund publication, based on J. Frederic Dewhurst's classic *America's Needs and Resources: A New Survey*. Many important charts, graphs, and statistics included.

105 U.S. Bureau of the Budget. The budget in brief. Govt. Print. Off. Annual. $.35.

In addition to this summary of the federal budget, every library should have copies of its state and local budgets, or at least abstracts of them, for the current year.

106 U.S. President. Economic report of the President transmitted to the Congress. . . . Govt. Print. Off., 1947– . Annual. $1.25.

An important document, not only for the up-to-date picture of the economy, but also for the invaluable statistical tables.

Directories

► Every reference collection should include the following basic tools, if they exist, for the library's own city, county, and state: alphabetical and classified telephone directories for local and adjacent areas; industrial directory for the city, county, or state; directory of directors of corporations for the local area; directory of labor unions for the local area.

107 American register of exporters and importers. American Register of Exporters and Importers Corp., Inc., 1946– . Annual. 1v. $15.

List of United States firms from which specific products may be purchased by foreign countries, arranged by product with alphabetical listing of exporters, importers, and export agents.

108 Editor and Publisher (Periodical). International yearbook number. Editor and Publisher, 1920–   . Annual (in Feb.). $10.

A geographical listing of newspapers, giving circulation and advertising information. Includes information on many foreign newspapers, national and press associations, Better Business Bureaus, awards, and many aspects of the newspaper industry.

109 Fortune (Periodical). Fortune directory of 500 largest U.S. industrial corporations. Fortune. Annual (in Aug.) $.50.

Actually a reprint from one of the issues of *Fortune*; includes also lists of largest banks, utilities, etc., as well as the 200 largest foreign industrials.

110 Klein, Bernard, ed. Guide to American directories: a guide to the major business directories of the United States, covering all industrial, professional and mercantile categories. 7th ed. Klein, 1967. 465p. $25.

A directory of directories. Arrangement is by subject, covering more than 300 categories. Under each entry there is descriptive information, price, and frequency of publication. Indexed also by name.

111 McNierney, Mary, ed. Directory of business and financial services. 6th ed. Special Libraries Assn., 1963. 187p. $6.50.

One of the important directories in the field. Selected list of business, economic, and financial publications which are printed periodically with regular supplements. Indexed by subject, and by publishers, services, and authors. Brief annotations, frequency of issue, and price included.

112 News Front (Periodical). 15,000 leading U.S. corporations. Year, Inc., 1966. 226p. $9.95. New edition will be published in fall of 1968: 25,000 leading U.S. corporations. $35.

Manufacturers, classified by industry categories, are ranked by annual sales and analyzed by 17 vital indexes, including sales, profits, assets, employees, plants, shares of the market, and diversification.

113 Thomas register of American manufacturers. Thomas Pub. Annual. 8v. v.1–6, Product classification; v.7, Alphabetical list of manufacturers; v.8, Product finding guide. $30.

National purchasing guide, supplying names and addresses of manufacturers, producers, importers, and other sources of supply in all lines and in all sections of the United States. Symbol showing minimum capital of each firm is given.

114 U.S. Labor Statistics Bureau. Directory of national and international labor unions in the United States. Govt. Print. Off., 1965. 100p. $.55.

Revised every two years, this is a good single title containing basic descriptive and statistical information pertaining to all aspects of unions.

115 U.S. Post Office Department. Directory of international mail. Govt. Print. Off., 1955–   . Irregular. 1v. $5 including binder; $2.50 without binder.

Rates governing mail to foreign countries, kept up to date with loose-leaf correction sheets.

116 ———National zip code directory. Govt. Print. Off., 1967–   . Annual. $7.

Compilation of zip code numbers for all addresses in the United States. When a new volume is ready, the old one will be replaced by the Post Office at no charge.

117 Wisdom, Donald F. Popular names of U.S. Government reports; a catalog. Govt. Print. Off., 1966. 32p. $.30.

118 World wide chamber of commerce directory. Johnson Publishing Co., Inc., 1967. 135p. Annual. $3.

Listing of chambers of commerce in the United States, including foreign chambers of commerce as well.

119 Zimmerman, Oswald Theodore, and Zimmerman, Mildred. College placement directory. 4th ed. Industrial Res. Ser., 1965. 643p. $16.

Gives in brief form much useful information about companies which employ college graduates, e.g., types of specialists employed, numbers employed each year, domestic and overseas employment, etc. Includes sections on government (federal, state, and city) employment, job classification, geographical distribution, a list of colleges with name of placement officer, Canadian colleges, and technical institutes. Indexed. Useful as a business directory as well as a guide to employment.

Dictionaries and Encyclopedias

120 Cyclopedia of insurance in the United States. Index Pub. Co., 1891–   . Annual. $8.75.

Lists insurance companies and organizations, important court decisions, definitions of insurance terms, forms, and biographical sketches of insurance officials. Includes a list of biographical sketches appearing in earlier volumes.

121 Encyclopedia of associations. 5th ed. Gale Res., 1968. v.1, National organizations of the U.S. 1231p. $29.50; v.2, Geographic and executive index (cumulated irregularly). $17.50; v.3, New associations and inter edition service (in prep.). Annual subscription. $25.

All types of national organizations are included: business, cultural, educational, fraternal, governmental, labor, religious, technical, and many others. Includes date of founding, description of activities, publications, and dates of annual meetings. Excellent indexes make the information easily available.

122 Exporters' encyclopaedia. Lowell Kerr, ed. Dun & Bradstreet, 1904–   . Annual. 1v. $50.

Full details for preparation of shipments to foreign countries, including supplementary bulletins to update information throughout the subscription year.

123 Heyel, Carl. Encyclopedia of management. Reinhold, 1963. 1084p. $27.50.

Covers such topics as work simplification, retirement plans, investment policy formulae, and many others. Arranged in dictionary form. Generally gives a definition and explanation of the topic, its history, a list of references for further information, and cross references.

124 Kohler, Eric Louis. A dictionary for accountants. 3d ed. Prentice-Hall, 1963. 523p. $14.95.

A standard work in the field, giving current definitions and information on more than 2600 terms in everyday language. Includes charts and forms when applicable.

125 Low, Janet. Investor's dictionary. Simon & Schuster, 1964. 217p. $4.95.

More simply written than the *Wall Street Thesaurus*. This is an excellent dictionary of many of the specialized terms used among investors. Definitions average about 100 words. Accurate, informative, and written with a light touch.

126 McGraw-Hill dictionary of modern economics. McGraw-Hill, 1965. 697p. $14.75.

An excellent dictionary. Can be used by students from high school up and by teachers and the general public. Definitions are simple enough for easy comprehension, but lengthy enough to include historical background information. Additional sources of information are given under each entry. Over 100 tables, charts, and diagrams supplement textual portions. Includes information on approximately 200 government and private agencies, organizations, and nonprofit associations concerned with economics and marketing.

127 Marshall, Henry. New business encyclopedia. Rev. ed. Doubleday, 1963. 526p. $4.95.

Covers a wide variety of subjects important to the householder as well as to the businessman: how to buy a house, how to get a job, how the services and publications of the Census Bureau can aid the businessman, marriage laws by states, divorce and separation grounds, facts for farmers, etc. In short, how to avoid costly business and legal errors. Many tables.

128 Munn, Glenn G. Encyclopedia of banking and finance. 6th ed. Bankers Pub., 1962. 788p. $25.

Essential function is to serve the banking, financial, and allied vocations by explanation and definition of terms in banking. Includes bibliographies. Alphabetically arranged; not too technical for the student.

Handbooks

129 Angel, Juvenal. International reference handbook of services, organizations, diplomatic representation, marketing and advertising channels. 4th ed. World Trade, 1965. 589p. $25.

An invaluable collection of basic information, covering a wide area of subjects. Arranged alphabetically by country; provides supplemental information about 120 foreign countries.

130 Aspley, John C. Sales manager's handbook. 10th ed. Dartnell Corp., 1965. 1007p. $19.50.

A classic in the field; each edition includes much new information, added to assist the manager on sales organization, training, methods of selling, and marketing research. Explanation of trade practices is an important feature.

131 ———Sales promotion handbook. 5th ed. Dartnell Corp., 1966. 1080p. $19.50.

Almost a companion volume to *Sales Manager's Handbook,* this title emphasizes sales techniques and promotion ideas.

132 Best's Insurance guide with key ratings . . . of all stock fire, marine, casualty and miscellaneous insurance companies operating in the United States . . . Best, 1906– . Annual. $11 (1967).

Supplies quick-reference key ratings and comprehensive statistics showing the financial condition, general standing, and transactions of various types of insurance companies.

133 Best's Life insurance reports . . . upon legal reserve companies, fraternal benefit societies and assessment associations operating in the United States. Best, 1906– . Annual. $40.
Gives complete, up-to-date information concerning all life-insurance carriers.

134 Croner's Reference book for world traders. Croner Pub., 1967. 380p. $18 a year.
Loose-leaf handbook of useful facts about trading requirements of specific countries. Lists trade organizations, credit information agencies, banks, customs brokers, advertising agencies, etc. Kept up to date by supplementary sheets.

135 Dartnell Corporation. Dartnell international trade handbook, by Gerard R. Richter and others. Leslie L. Lewis, ed. 2d ed. Dartnell Corp., 1965. 1023p. $17.50.
Full and up-to-date treatment of the principles underlying all aspects of foreign trade. Includes appendix of such ready-reference information as abbreviations, allowances for foreign travel, and conversion tables. Selected bibliography.

136 Economic almanac. Nat. Ind. Conf. Bd., 1940– . Biennial. $9.95.
Handbook of useful facts about business, labor, and government in the United States, Canada, and other world areas. Some topics discussed are prices, savings, standards of living, foreign trade, and wages. Glossary of selected terms used in economic and business reports. Less general and more practical for management than the *Statistical Abstract of the U.S.*

137 Editor and publisher market guide. Editor and Publisher, 1924– . Annual. $10.
Arrangement is by state and city, giving, under each city, its population, location, trade areas, banks, climate, principal

industries, colleges and universities, largest department stores, newspapers, etc.

138 Frey, Albert W. Marketing handbook. 2d ed. Ronald, 1965. Various paging. $15.

A guide for everyone concerned with selling and marketing goods and services. Modeled after the original *Marketing Handbook,* this book includes statistical and mathematical tools, law of sales, and service policies, plus the usual marketing subjects.

139 Hodgson, Richard S. Dartnell direct mail and mail order handbook. Dartnell Corp., 1964. 1092p. $19.50.

An encyclopedic single volume which covers all aspects of the subject. Includes a basic list of business directories, code of ethics, and postal rates and regulations.

140 Hutchinson, Lois. Standard handbook for secretaries. 7th ed. McGraw-Hill, 1956. 638p. $6.95.

The accepted basic title in the field. Index is particularly good because of its great detail. In addition to excellent office-practice information, the sections on English grammar, choice of words, and punctuation are invaluable.

141 Lasser, J. K. Handbook of accounting methods. 3d ed. Van Nostrand, 1964. 970p. $16.50.

Gives details of handling accounting problems in more than 60 different industries, with automatic data processing included where pertinent.

142 Lasser (J. K.) Institute. Your income tax. Simon & Schuster, 1937–   . Annual. $1.95.

Designed to facilitate preparation of income-tax returns. Includes sample forms. Indexed.

143 McMichael, Stanley L. McMichael's Appraising manual. 4th ed. Prentice-Hall, 1951. 731p. $8.95.

Methods of appraisal described in detail with numerous

illustrations, including farm, residential, and business properties. Many useful tables. Indispensable for any large real-estate operator.

144 National Industrial Conference Board. Expenditure patterns of the American family. Fabian Linden, ed. The Board, 1965. 175p. $25.

"This study contains the most comprehensive collection of information on consumer expenditure that has ever been assembled." A remarkable study sponsored by *Life,* prepared by NICB, and based on a survey conducted by the U.S. Department of Labor.

145 Office management handbook. Edited by Harry L. Wylie. Staff ed., James Q. Harty. 2d ed. Ronald, 1958. 890p. $14.

Developed under the auspices of the National Office Management Association, this is a comprehensive treatment of all the important aspects of office operations. Illustrations.

146 Scott Publications, Inc. Scott's Standard postage stamp catalogue. Scott Publications, 1868–   . Annual. 1v. $13.50 in 1966.

Gives minute details—such as date of issue, design, denomination, color, perforation, and watermark—on all the stamps of the world. Most of the stamps are priced. Illustrated.

147 Taintor, Sarah A., and Monro, K. M. Secretary's handbook, a manual of correct usage. 8th ed. Macmillan, 1958. 559p. $5.95.

Published since 1929, this has been a classic handbook for a long time. Covers problems of writing for the most part, with many examples of types of letters. Not quite so detailed on grammar as Hutchinson's *Standard Handbook for Secretaries.* A valuable title in the field.

148 U.S. Internal Revenue Service. Your federal income tax for individuals. Govt. Print. Off. Annual. $.50.

Useful booklet designed to help taxpayers prepare their tax

returns. Simply written, it explains in detail what can and cannot be deducted, etc.

Yearbooks

149 Commodity yearbook. Commodity Research Bureau, 1939– . $16.95.

Background data and statistical history of more than 100 basic commodities and special commodity studies. A good quick-reference source.

150 International Trade Review (Periodical). World trade data yearbook. Dun & Bradstreet. $5.

Authoritative information on advertising, transportation, sales, and financial aspects of world trade. January issue of *International Trade Review*.

151 Sales Management (Periodical). Survey of buying power. Sales Management, 1929– . Annual. $6.

Published as an issue of the periodical, this is one of the definitive surveys of population, effective buying income, and retail sales. Additional statistical estimates included.

6
Social Sciences

General

Bibliographies

152 White, Carl Milton, and others, eds. Sources of information in the social sciences; a guide to the literature. Bedminster Pr., 1964. 498p. $10.50.

An annotated guide to the mass of literature in the social science field. Arranged in eight broad categories. Author and title index.

Dictionaries and Encyclopedias

153 Encyclopedia of social work. Nat. Assn. of Social Workers, 1965– . 1060p. $13.

A successor to the *Social Work Year Book,* to be published at appropriate intervals. In addition to various topical articles by specialists, it has a listing of international and national governmental and voluntary agencies, including officials, membership, purpose, activities, periodicals, etc.

154 Encyclopedia of the social sciences. Editor in chief, Edwin R. A. Seligman. Macmillan, 1937. 8v. $37.50 each; $169.95 the set.

In parts outdated, but still a comprehensive encyclopedia of the whole field of the social sciences, prepared by top authorities in the fields. The new 17-volume *International Encyclopedia of the Social Sciences* does not supersede this set.

155 Gould, Julius, and Kolb, W. L., eds. A dictionary of the social sciences. Compiled under the auspices of the United Nations Educational, Scientific, and Cultural Organization. Free Pr., 1964. 761p. $19.50.

Definitions and historical background for terms. Signed articles with good cross references.

155a International encyclopedia of the social sciences. Macmillan, 1968. 17v. $495.

An important and valuable addition to this subject area. Originally planned as a new edition of the *Encyclopedia of the Social Sciences,* but, as completed, it is an entirely new work. Articles signed. Selected bibliographies and a comprehensive index are included.

Directories

156 Foundation directory. 3d ed. Russell Sage, 1967. 1198p. $12.

Lists 6803 nongovernmental, nonprofit organizations having principal assets of $200,000 or distributing annually $10,000 or more in grants or for program. The donor, officers and trustees, purpose, activities, financial status, and grants made are given for each organization. Arranged by state. Separate indexes for fields of interest, persons, and foundations.

Social Services

Directories

157 American Foundation for the Blind, Inc. Directory of agencies serving blind persons in the United States. 14th ed. The Foundation, 1965. 234p. $4.

A useful guide to state and local agencies. Includes lists of specialized agencies in Section 2.

158 American Public Welfare Association. Public welfare directory, 1966. The Association, 1966. 232p. $15.

A comprehensive list of federal, state, and local public assistance and welfare agencies, including officials. Material on "Where to write" for vital records. Not an annual. Correction notices issued frequently.

159 Hospitals (Periodical). Hospitals; guide issue. Am. Hospital Assn., 1945– . Annual. $3.50.

Part 2 of the August issue of the periodical, *Hospitals,* contains a directory of registered hospitals and information on the American Hospital Association, government agencies, and professional schools. Includes also detailed hospital statistics and a guide for hospital buyers.

160 National Association for Mental Health, Inc. Directory of resources for mentally ill children in the United States, 1964. The Association, 1964. 96p. Paper $2.

This directory lists, by state, all available facilities for mentally ill children. Includes name of director, staffing pattern, fees, and other significant facets of these important services.

The Negro

161 Davis, John Preston, ed. American Negro reference book.
Prentice-Hall, 1966. 969p. $22.50.
  Extensive and complete reference book, covering every major
aspect of Negro life in America from colonial times to the
present. Bibliographies and tables for most chapters. Well indexed.

162 Ebony (Periodical). Negro handbook. Johnson Pub. Co.,
1966. 535p. $12.50.
  Includes a biographical dictionary. Has in appendixes a
directory of Negroes holding elective or appointive positions in
state, municipal, and county agencies, 1965, and a list of organizations. Indexed. Complements *The American Negro Reference Book.*

163 Ploski, Harry A., and Brown, Roscoe C. Negro almanac;
the Negro, his part in America. Bellwether Publishing Co.,
1967. 1012p. $22.
  Useful work containing excellent biographical material. Arranged in four sections: I, Chronology 1492–1966; II, Significant documents in American history; III, Historical landmarks
of Negro Americans; IV, Civil rights organizations and their
leadership, past and present.

Statistics

Yearbooks

164 Almanack, by Joseph Whitaker. Whitaker, 1869–   . Annual. $6.50.
  Similar to *World Almanac,* this annual contains an enormous
amount of statistical and descriptive information concerning
Great Britain, plus brief information for other parts of the
world. Detailed index.

165 Canadian almanac and directory. Copp, 1847–   . Annual.
$12.50.

Statistical and directory material relating to Canada.

166 Information please almanac. Simon & Schuster, 1947– .
Annual. $2.95; paper $1.50.
Many facts assembled for quick reference. Needed even if
World Almanac is purchased, for each volume contains some
material not found in the other.

167 Reader's Digest almanac. Reader's Digest; for sale by Little,
1966– . Annual. $2.50; paper $1.75.
A useful compilation of facts, figures, dates, names, etc.,
arranged in 20 broad topics. Good index.

168 South American handbook. Rand McNally, 1924– . An-
nual. $6.95.
A yearbook and guide to the countries and resources of South
America, Central America, Mexico, Caribbean, and West
Indies.

169 Statesman's year-book; statistical and historical annual of
the states of the world. Rev. after official returns. Macmillan,
1864– . Annual. $10.
Excellent, concise yearbook giving detailed information concerning constitution and government, economic conditions, commerce, agriculture, religion, etc., of the governments of the
world. Bibliographies of reference books for each country. Particularly good for Great Britain and members of the Commonwealth. Indexed.

170 United Nations. Statistical Office. Demographic yearbook.
U.N. Publications, 1949– . Annual. $15; paper $11.
Official compilation of international demographic data in
such fields as area and population, natality, mortality, marriage, divorce, international migration, etc.

171 World almanac and book of facts. Newspaper Enterprise
Assn., Inc., 1868– . Annual. $2.75.
A ready-reference tool containing much statistical material

for the current and preceding years; important events of the year; associations, societies, and their addresses; and many other items.

Statistics—United States

172 U.S. Bureau of the Census. Census of population: 1960. Govt. Print. Off., 1961–64. For prices, see note below.

This is a part of the 18th decennial census. Volume I, Characteristics of the Population, was issued in 58 parts. Volume I, Part 1, is the U.S. Summary, $6.25. Parts 2–57 cover the individual states, District of Columbia, and outlying areas. Each library will want the part covering its own state and possibly those for some adjoining states. Pages and prices vary with the size of the state, e.g., New York State, pt.34, 951p., $6.50. The price of the complete Volume I is $236.75. If other census volumes are needed, a Price List may be secured from the Superintendent of Documents without charge.

173 County and city data book, 1967. Govt. Print. Off., 1967. 673p. $5.50.

This volume provides, for convenient reference, a selection of recent statistical information for counties, cities, and other relatively small areas. Supplements the *Statistical Abstract*. A new volume is prepared at intervals to reflect latest census findings.

174 ———Historical statistics of the United States, colonial times to 1957. Govt. Print. Off., 1964. 789p. $6.

A valuable compilation of many important statistics taken from census records. This work supplies, for many items, a retrospective record of data formerly furnished in the *Statistical Abstract*.

175 ———Historical statistics of the United States, colonial times to 1957. Continuation to 1962 and revisions. Govt. Print. Off., 1965. 154p. $1.

To be used in conjunction with *Historical Statistics of the United States* (above).

176 ———Statistical abstract of the United States. Govt. Print. Off., 1879– . Annual. $3.75 (1966), $4 (1967).

An important collection of statistical data culled from the reports of agencies of the United States. Usually gives some retrospective statistics.

Politics and Government

Dictionaries

177 Plano, Jack Charles, and Greenberg, Milton. American political dictionary. Rev. and enl. ed. Holt, 1967. 401p. $6.95; paper $4.95.

The vocabulary of government institutions, practices, and traditions, at the federal, state, and local level.

Yearbooks

178 International year book and statesmen's who's who. Burke's Peerage, 1953– . Annual. $28.

Information on the economic and political structure of each country in the world, followed by the biographies of the principal persons in each country.

179 Political handbook and atlas of the world; parliaments, parties, and press . . . Council on Foreign Relations, Inc. (Harper), 1927– . Annual. $8.50 (1966 ed.).

Gives chief government officials, political parties, their leaders and programs, political events, names of newspapers, their proprietors and editors. Must be kept up to date from newspapers.

Miscellaneous

180 Marx, Karl, and Engels, F. Communist manifesto. Affiliated

Pub. Washington Square, 1965. 158p. $3.95.

Continuing demand from students makes it advisable to include a reference copy of this document.

Politics and Government—United States

181 Ogg, Frederic Austin, and Ray, Perley 'Orman. Ogg and Ray's Introduction to American government, by William H. Young. 13th ed. Appleton, 1966. 979p. $8.75.

Standard text, giving an excellent account of the foundations of the United States government; National government; State government; and Local government. Well indexed.

182 Porter, Kirk H., and Johnson, Donald Bruce, comps. National party platforms, 1840–1964. 3d ed. Univ. of Illinois Pr., 1966. 698p. $10.75.

Texts of the platforms of major and minor parties are included in this collection, which goes back to the very beginnings of these important political statements.

183 U.S. Congress. Senate. Library. Nomination and election of the President and Vice President of the United States, including manner of selecting delegates to national political conventions. Govt. Print. Off., 1964. 239p. $.75.

A convenient explanation of procedures.

184 U.S. Laws, statutes, etc. U.S. code. 1964 ed. containing the general and permanent laws of the United States in force on January 3, 1965. Prepared and published . . . by the Committee on the Judiciary of the House of Representatives. Govt. Print. Off., 1964. 14v. $87.25 the set. 1st supplement, 1965. $6.75.

Although the medium-sized public library cannot satisfy all the needs of the legal specialist, it is important to supply the codified laws of the United States. Similarly, most libraries will need the codified laws of their own states.

185 U.S. President. Inaugural addresses of the Presidents of the United States from George Washington, 1789, to Lyndon B.

Johnson, 1965. Comp. by the Legislative Reference Service. Govt. Print. Off., 1965. 274p. $1.25.

A convenient compilation for reference.

Directories

186 Book of the states. Council of State Governments, 1935– . Biennial with supplements. $12.

In addition to general articles on various aspects of state government, provides many statistical and directory data, and the nickname, motto, flower, bird, song, and chief officials of each state. The supplements list latest elective officials and legislators.

187 Municipal year book; an authoritative résumé of activities and statistical data of American cities. Int. City Managers. 1934– . Annual. $12.

Very complete statistical data, combined with current information on individual city programs. Information on urban counties and metropolitan areas. Includes directory of city officials.

188 U.S. Congress. . . . Official Congressional directory for the use of the U.S. Congress. . . . Govt. Print. Off., 1809– . Annual. $3.50.

Complete listing of organization and members of Congress, including biographical sketches, Congressional committees, commissions, boards, and departments; also information on the judiciary, diplomats and consular service, press and other galleries, and small maps showing congressional districts. Indexed.

189 U.S. Congress. House. Committee on Un-American Activities. Guide to subversive organizations and publications. Govt. Print. Off., 1961. 248p. $.70.

Lists organizations and publications cited as Communist by federal authorities and state investigating committees, and organizations designated by U.S. attorneys general as Fascist or otherwise extremist in character. Excerpts from Communist, etc., citations are given. Separate indexes of persons, organizations, and publications.

190 United States government organization manual. Govt. Print. Off., 1935–   . Annual. $2.

Most important annually revised source of information on all government agencies, giving history, organization authority, activities, and chief officials with organizational charts. Also lists agencies abolished, transferred, and terminated. Index of names as well as general index.

Constitution

191 Constitution of the United States of America, analysis and interpretation. Govt. Print. Off., 1964. 1693p. $15.50.

Contains annotations of Supreme Court decisions through June 22, 1964, and provides the current operative meaning of all articles of the Constitution.

192 Cushman, Robert Eugene, and Cushman, Robert F. Cases in constitutional law. 2d ed. Appleton, 1963. 945p. $8.95.

A comprehensive collection of important Supreme Court decisions, for the student of American constitutional law. Each case is preceded by an explanatory comment.

193 Cushman, Robert Eugene. Leading constitutional decisions. 13th ed. Appleton, 1966. 585p. Paper $3.95.

A collection of the most important Supreme Court decisions on constitutional questions of lasting importance through the fall of 1962, for the use of students of American government and American history.

Law

194 Kling, Samuel G. Complete guide to everyday law. Follett, 1966. 624p. $6.95.

A layman's guide to basic legal questions covering marriage

and divorce, wills, contracts, social security, legal forms, lawyer's fees, and many other important topics in clear question-and-answer method.

Parliamentary Procedure

195 Robert, Henry Martyn. Rules of order, revised. (75th anniversary ed.) Scott, 1951. 326p. $3.75.

A compendium of parliamentary law, explaining methods of organizing and conducting the business of societies, conventions, and other assemblies.

Armed Services

196 Army Times (Periodical). Guide to Army posts. 2d ed. Stackpole, 1966. 383p. $4.95.

Directory of United States Army stations around the world, including rules for easier living on and around them.

197 Uniforms of the United States Army. Barnes (Encore reprint), 1959. 2v. v.1, $17.95; v.2, $14.95.

Volume 1 by H. L. Nelson; Volume 2 by Martin Pakula. A reprint of the famous paintings of the United States Army uniforms from the earliest days to 1907.

198 U.S. Department of Defense. A dictionary of United States military terms, prepared for joint usage of the Armed Services by the Joint Chiefs of Staff. Public Affairs Press, 1963. 316p. $4.50.

Lists thousands of military terms, many of which have come into wide usage since World War II.

International Relations

199 Annuaire des organisations internationales. Yearbook of international organizations. Int. Pub. Ser., 1948– . Biennial. $20.

An encyclopedic dictionary of international organizations and

associations currently active; their functions, officers, their abbreviations, aims, finance, activities, and publications.

200 Council on Foreign Relations, Inc. American agencies interested in international affairs. 5th rev. ed. Pub. for The Council,
by Praeger, 1964. 200p. $5.50.

"A description of those private organizations which conduct
serious programs of research in international affairs or which
maintain meetings and information programs on a continuing
basis."—*Preface*. Gives purpose, organization, finance, staff,
activities, membership, membership fees, and publications for
each organization.

201 Everyman's United Nations; the structure, functions and
work of the organization and its related agencies during the
years 1945–1962, and a United Nations chronology for 1963.
7th ed. United Nations. Office of Information, 1964. 638p. $5.

A first purchase for general information about the United
Nations.

202 United Nations. Yearbook. Columbia Univ. Pr. in cooperation with the United Nations, 1946/47–   . Annual. $21.50
(1965).

An annual summary of the activities of the constituent bodies
and specialized agencies of the United Nations. Subject and
name indexes.

Etiquette

203 Post, Emily (Price). Etiquette; the blue book of social usage.
11th ed. Funk, 1960. 671p. $6.95.

Although the Vanderbilt *New Complete Book of Etiquette*
covers every topic in manners and social behavior, there is still
demand for "Emily Post," especially for formal occasions. Both
volumes are recommended for all libraries.

204 Vanderbilt, Amy. New complete book of etiquette; the guide

to gracious living. New rev. ed. Doubleday, 1963. 738p. $5.50.
Well adapted to the fashions and customs of modern life. It
covers in detail every facet of social behavior and manners in
today's world.

Holidays

205 Douglas, George William. The American book of days; a
compendium of information about holidays, festivals, notable
anniversaries and Christian and Jewish holy days, with notes
on other American anniversaries worthy of remembrance. 2d
ed. rev. by Helen Douglas Compton. Wilson, 1948. 697p. $8.
   Arrangement is chronological. Descriptive account of important days in secular and religious life.

206 Hazeltine, Mary Emogene. Anniversaries and holidays; a
calendar of days and how to observe them. 2d ed. comp. rev.
with the editorial assistance of Judith K. Sollenberger. American
Library Assn., 1944. 316p. $6.
   Although this book is now twenty years old, it affords a comprehensive record of important dates in calendar-year order.
Includes many bibliographical references.

207 Spicer, Dorothy Gladys. Festivals of Western Europe. Wilson, 1958. 275p. $5.
   Descriptive material on the principal festivals of Belgium,
Denmark, France, Germany, Italy, Luxembourg, The Nether-
lands, Norway, Portugal, Spain, Sweden, and Switzerland. Contains a table of Easter dates and movable festivals dependent
upon Easter, 1958–87 inclusive; a glossary of festival terms;
bibliography; and indexes of festivals by name and by country.

7
Education

Dictionaries and Encyclopedias

▶ There is no general encyclopedia of education currently in print comparable to the classic Monroe work now over fifty years old: Monroe, Paul, ed. Cyclopedia of education. Macmillan, 1911–13. 5v. in 3.

208 Encyclopedia of educational research; a project of the American Educational Research Association. Edited by Chester W. Harris. 3d ed. Macmillan, 1960. 1564p. $27.50.

Summarizes and critically evaluates reported research in many areas of education. Each topic includes a bibliography. More recent research may be followed in the *Review of Educational Research,* a periodical published under the same auspices.

209 Good, Carter Victor, ed. Dictionary of education. 2d ed. McGraw-Hill, 1959. 676p. $11.50.

A comprehensive dictionary of technical and professional terms and concepts. Excludes names of persons, institutions, school systems, and places except when a movement, method, or plan is represented. Includes foreign educational terms most frequently employed in the study of comparative education. Pronunciation is given for difficult and foreign language words and for medical and psychological terms.

Directories

210 American Council on Education. American junior colleges. 7th ed. Edited by Edmund J. Gleazer, Jr. The Council, 1967. 957p. $14.

Information on 751 accredited junior colleges, usually revised every four years. Pattern is similar to that of *American Universities and Colleges,* to which this book is a companion volume. In addition to all the usual data, it includes each college's programs of study for transfer to senior colleges, as well as those for terminal or vocational-technical courses. Appendixes include information on regional accrediting agencies, off-campus housing, curricula, admission, church-related colleges, and changes since 6th edition.

211 ———American universities and colleges. 9th ed. Edited by Allan M. Cartter. The Council, 1964. 1339p. $15.

An encyclopedic work on higher education, usually revised every four years. Part I gives an overview of the field, including college admissions, history and structure of higher education, relationship to the federal government, and the foreign student in the United States. Part II covers professional education. Part III, the main part, lists colleges and universities by state. For each it includes type, history, requirements, fees, departments and staff, distinctive programs and activities, degrees, enrollment, foreign students, library, publications, student aid, finances, buildings and grounds, and administrative officers. Appendixes include information on accreditation, academic costume, degree abbreviations, earned doctorates conferred 1861–1962, and ROTC units.

212 Baird, William R. Baird's Manual of American college fraternities. 17th ed. Banta, 1963. 834p. $8.

Histories, including chapter lists, of undergraduate and professional-school fraternities and honor societies. Also lists campuses and their fraternities.

213 Cass, James, and Birnbaum, Max. Comparative guide to American colleges for students, parents and counselors. New and enl. ed. Harper, 1965. 725p. $9.95; paper $3.95.

Differs from most college directories by giving a profile of each institution, including academic atmosphere of campus and percent of applicants admitted. Its Selectivity Index ranks institutions by the academic potential of their student bodies. Also contains a list of public institutions that accept out-of-state students, and a list of institutions conferring the largest number of degrees in selected fields.

214 College Entrance Examination Board. College handbook. Educational Testing Service, 1941–   . Biennial. 902p. $3.50 (1967–69).

Limited to member institutions of the College Entrance Examination Board, all of which are fully accredited. Includes basic information such as location, size, programs of study, terms of admission, annual expenses, financial aid, and where to write for further information.

215 Directory for exceptional children. 5th ed. Sargent, 1965. 702p. $7.

Designed to encompass all facilities for training, rehabilitation, therapy, and education of children unacceptable to, or unable to benefit fully from, regular schools. Answers queries of doctors, social workers, counselors, and parents. Excludes programs for the gifted.

216 Educators guide to free films. Educators Progress Service, 1941–   . Annual. $9.50.

Alphabetical listing of free films under each of 30 curriculum areas. Entries include technical description, annotation, and source. Separate indexes for titles, subjects, and sources.

217 Educators guide to free filmstrips. Educators Progress Service, 1949–   . Annual. $7.

Similar in format to *Educators Guide to Free Films*.

218 The gifted: educational resources. Sargent, 1964. 285p. $4.

Information on private and public schools which place special emphasis on realizing the capabilities of mentally superior students. Also includes colleges and universities offering courses for teachers of the gifted, and an inventory of programs for superior students in American colleges and universities.

219 Handbook of private schools, an annual descriptive survey

of independent education. Sargent, 1915– . Annual. $10.

Long recognized as the principal directory of private schools, the 1966 edition being the 47th. Gives the following data, for both boarding and day schools: type, director, admissions officer, curriculum, date established, school calendar, admissions, enrollment, faculty, graduates, tuition, summer session, plant evaluation, and endowment. Also includes tutorial and remedial schools.

220 Hawes, Gene R. New American guide to colleges. 3d ed. Columbia Univ. Pr., 1966. 597p. $8.95.

Attempts to give the kind of information which will simplify the selection of colleges to which to apply. Arrangement is by type of college, e.g., co-ed, state, liberal arts, etc. Facts are supplied under the following general headings: general character of the college; student life; degrees, programs of study, and academic character; tuition and boarding charges, scholarships, and other financial aid; admissions policies and levels of academic demands; enrollment and graduate schools. College Discovery Index is a special feature.

221 Lovejoy, Clarence Earle. Lovejoy's Career and vocational school guide; a source book, clue book and directory of job training opportunities. 3d enl. ed. comp. rev. Simon & Schuster, 1967. 176p. $6.50; paper $3.95.

A comprehensive guide to the expanding field of vocational education, including a detailed listing of training programs in the armed services, apprenticeship programs, and home-study courses. Directory section includes schools which offer training in trades and technologies, airline jobs, medical and health services, performing arts, etc. All schools listed were resurveyed for this edition.

222 ———Lovejoy's Scholarship guide. Simon & Schuster, 1964. 91 p. $4.95; paper $2.95.

Guide to scholarships, loans, and part-time jobs. Simpler and less detailed than Feingold.

223 ———comp. Lovejoy's College guide. 9th ed. Simon & Schuster, 1967. 416p. $6.50; paper $3.95.

The most-asked-for guide to colleges. Part I is an orientation, for parents and prospective students, to virtually all aspects of college: costs, admissions, religious affiliations and activities, etc. Part II explains accreditation and symbols used to classify colleges, lists colleges according to career curricula, and provides rating and description of institutions which form the major part of the guide. Frequently revised.

224 Patterson's American education. Educational Directories, Inc., 1904– . Annual. $25.

A comprehensive directory of educational institutions, including state departments of education, public school systems, private and denominational schools, special schools, colleges, and universities. Arranged by state, then by town, and by classification of speciality. Also includes educational associations and societies.

225 Study abroad; international guide fellowships, scholarships, educational exchange, 1966–68. UNESCO, 1966. Biennial. $4.

Information on more than 170,000 individual opportunities for study and educational travel abroad. Companion volume is UNESCO *Handbook of International Exchange,* which gives information on more than 5300 agencies and organizations conducting programs of international exchange and cultural cooperation. Arranged by field of study, type of program, and country.

226 U.S. Office of Education. Directory. Part 1, State governments; Part 2, Public school systems by state, and cities, with name of superintendent, local zip code, county enrollment, and grade span; Part 3, Higher education; Part 4, Education associations; Part 5, Federal government. Govt. Print. Off., 1912– . Annual. Nominal cost for each part: $.60; $1.50; $1.00; $.55; $.25.

Inexpensive compilation of facts on the structure of educational systems and names of officials for the entire United States.

Handbooks

227 American Council on Education. Commission on Plans and Objectives for Higher Education. An assessment of quality in graduate education, by Allan M. Cartter. The Council, 1966. 131p. $5; paper $3.

Ranks leading university departments by the quality of the faculty and effectiveness of the programs. Arranged by fields of study, e.g., humanities, social sciences, biological sciences, physical sciences, and engineering.

228 Feingold, S. Norman. Scholarships, fellowships and loans. Bellman. v.3, 1955; v.4, 1962. $10 each.

Comprehensive coverage of the field, listed by administering agency with indexes by name of scholarship, fellowship, or loan and by vocational goals or fields of interest. Volumes 1 and 2 are out of print. Volumes 3 and 4 cover the ground effectively in themselves. Volume 3 contains master index to Volumes 1, 2, and 3; Volume 4 contains index to Volumes 3 and 4.

229 U.S. Civil Service Commission. Federal career directory; a guide for college students. Govt. Print. Off., 1966. 88p. $.55.

A working tool for the college student and the counselor. Divided into three parts: general discussion on federal employment, federal agencies and their programs, and job briefs for major categories of jobs. Well illustrated.

230 U.S. Office of Education. Division of Educational Statistics. Digest of educational statistics. Govt. Print. Off., 1962– . Annual. $1.

Statistical summary of elementary, secondary, and higher education in the United States, both public and nonpublic. Contains many useful tables and an index.

231 Woellner, Elizabeth H., and Wood, M. Aurilla. Require-

ments for certification of teachers, counselors, librarians, and administrators for elementary schools, secondary schools, junior colleges. Univ. of Chicago Pr., 1935– . Annual. Paper $3.75.

Provides detailed minimum requirements for certification by semester hours. Arrangement is by state. Important to have latest edition.

8
Science and Technology

Science—General

Bibliographies and Indexes

232 Applied science and technology index. Wilson, 1958– . Monthly except Aug. Annual cumulations. Service basis.

An index, by subject only, to approximately 225 periodicals in the fields of aeronautics, automation, chemistry, construction, electricity and electronics, engineering, geology and metallurgy, industrial and mechanical arts, machinery, physics, telecommunication, transportation, and related areas. Established in 1958 when *Industrial Arts Index* was divided into two separate indexes: *Applied Science and Technology Index* and *Business Periodicals Index*.

233 Bennett, Melvin. Science and technology: a purchase guide for branch and small public libraries. Carnegie Lib., Pittsburgh, 1963. 64p. $4.50. Annual supplements, 1963– . 1963, 42p. $1; 1964, 48p. $1.25; 1965, 112p. $2.50; 1966, 96p. $1.50.

Arranged by author. Includes publisher, date of publication, price, Dewey classification number, brief annotation, and a list of out-of-print books.

234 Biological and agricultural index. Wilson, 1964– . Monthly except Sept. Cumulated. Service basis.

Prior to 1964, was called the *Agricultural Index*. A detailed alphabetical subject index to agricultural, biological, and related periodicals in the English language.

235 Deason, Hilary J., ed. A guide to science reading. New Amer. Lib., 1966. 288p. Paper $.75.

A selective annotated bibliography, listed by Dewey classes. Four introductory essays by authorities in the field preface each list. Intended for use as a popular guide for the student and the layman. Supplemented by a quarterly periodical, *Science Books* (1965–   ).

236 McGraw-Hill basic bibliography of science and technology. McGraw-Hill, 1966. 738p. $19.50.

Lists books (nonbook materials are not included) under the headings used in the *McGraw-Hill Encyclopedia of Science and Technology,* giving one or more annotated citations for each topic. In the case of very specialized topics, the reader is referred to a related, more general heading for references bearing on his fields of interest. The topical guide organizes the 7400 subject headings into about 100 broad areas under which the reader can find particular subject headings in his field of interest. Throughout the volume, there are many cross references to related titles. Most useful when used with the *Encyclopedia,* to which this volume is a supplement.

237 Sarton, George. A guide to the history of science. Ronald, 1952. 316p. $7.50.

In two parts: Part I, History of science; Part II, History of science in special countries and of special sciences. Lists journals and serials concerning the history and philosophy of science; national and international organizations; institutions, museums and libraries; international congresses, and prizes pertaining to the history of science.

Dictionaries, Directories, and Encyclopedias

238 De Vries, Louis. French-English science dictionary. 3d ed. McGraw-Hill, 1962. 655p. $10.50.

Lists about 50,000 entries covering most sciences. Hundreds of idioms, mostly based on verb forms, and a revised supplement of terms in aeronautics, electronics, radar, radio, television, atomic energy, and nuclear science are also included. A grammatical guide for translators has been added.

239 German-English science dictionary. 3d ed. including supplement. McGraw-Hill, 1959. 592p. $7.

Includes more than 50,000 terms, chiefly technical. A new section on Suggestions for Translators has been added to this edition.

240 Harper encyclopedia of science. Edited by James R. Newman. Rev. ed. Harper, 1967. 1379p. $35.

A useful science encyclopedia for the layman. Contains nearly 4000 signed articles on the physical sciences, mathematics, biology, logic, and the history and philosophy of science. Extensive index, biographies, numerous illustrations, and a classified bibliography. The 1967 edition contains the text of the four-volume 1963 edition with some changes and new articles.

241 McGraw-Hill encyclopedia of science and technology: an international reference work. Rev. ed. David I. Eggenberger, executive ed. 15v. McGraw-Hill, 1966. $295; to schools and libraries, $229.50.

242 Annual supplement: McGraw-Hill yearbook of science and technology, 1962–1967. $24.

Useful for all levels of readers and in all types of libraries where there is need for authoritative, well-written, clearly explained, and suitably illustrated scientific-technical information. Represented are all the natural sciences and all their major applications in agriculture, engineering, forestry, and food technologies, but not psychiatry or clinical medicine.

243 Scientific and technical societies of the United States and Canada. 7th ed. National Academy of Sciences—National Research Council, 1961. 413, 54p. $9.

Lists professional and selected amateur societies. Address, names of officers, history, purpose, professional activities, number of members, titles of publications, and number of meetings a year are given for each society. Separate sections for the United States and for Canada, and separate indexes for each country.

Handbooks

244 Hiscox, Gardner Dexter, ed. Henley's Twentieth century book of formulas. Rev. 1956 by Harry E. Eisenson; new rev. and enl. ed. by T. O'Conor Sloane. Books, 1957. 867p. $5.

First published in 1937. Contains 10,000 selected formulas for household, workshop, and scientific applications, as well as recipes, processes, and money-saving ideas for both the amateur and the professional worker. Good index.

Natural Sciences

Astronomy

245 Flammarion, Camille. Flammarion book of astronomy. Simon & Schuster, 1964. 670p. $22.95.

A geocentric essay on astronomy chiefly concerned with the solar system and the stars. Contains sections on astrophysics, extragalactic nebulae, telescopes, artificial satellites, and space vehicles. Well illustrated and indexed.

246 Menzel, Donald Howard. A field guide to the stars and planets, including the moon, satellites, comets, and other features of the universe. Houghton, 1964. 397p. $4.95.

A useful handbook for both the layman and the professional astronomer. Clearly written, well illustrated, with a glossary of astronomical terms and adequate index.

247 Norton, Arthur Philip. A star atlas and reference handbook (epoch 1950) for students and amateurs. 15th ed. Gall, 1964. 58p. $4.90.

Covers the whole star sphere; shows more than 9000 stars,

nebulae, and clusters. Provides descriptive tests of objects mostly suitable for viewing through small telescopes. Notes on planets and star nomenclature are included.

Biology

248 Altman, Philip L., and Dittmer, Dorothy S., eds. Biological data book. Federation of American Societies for Experimental Biology, 1964. 633p. $10.

A basic reference for biology, organized into quantitative and descriptive tables, charts, and diagrams. A large number of literature citations are included.

249 Gray, Peter, ed. Encyclopedia of the biological sciences. Reinhold, 1961. 1119p. $20.

More than 800 signed articles written by specialists, covering the developmental, ecological, functional, genetic, structural, and taxonomic aspects of the biological sciences. Long, detailed articles not only define, explain, and describe their subject, but also offer additional reference sources. A well-designed reference tool for a broad audience that can range from the high school biology student to the practicing biologist. Adequately illustrated. Indexed.

250 Henderson, Isabella Ferguson, and Henderson, William Dawson. Dictionary of biological terms: pronunciation, derivation, and definition, of terms in biology, botany, zoology, anatomy, cytology, genetics, embryology, physiology. 8th ed. Edited by J. H. Kenneth. Van Nostrand, 1963. 640p. $12.50.

A basic tool, but does not include systematic names of plants and animals or references to term sources. Previous editions published with title *Dictionary of Scientific Terms*.

Botany

251 Mathews, Ferdinand Schuyler. Field book of American wild flowers. Edited by Norman Taylor. Rev. and enl. ed. Putnam, 1955. 601p. $5.95.

A useful guide to the flowers found east of the Rockies. Illustrations are ample and adequate.

252 Petrides, George A. A field guide to trees and shrubs; field marks of all trees, shrubs, and woody vines that grow wild in the Northeastern and North-Central United States and in southeastern and south-central Canada. Houghton, 1958. 431p. $4.95.

An adequate guide to the trees, shrubs, and vines of the Northeast.

Chemistry and Physics

253 Callaham, Ludmilla Ignatiev. Russian-English chemical and polytechnical dictionary. 2d ed. Wiley, 1962. 892p. $19.50.

A substantial technical dictionary which includes a general vocabulary of terms likely to appear in the technical literature. Contains many Russian terms selected from new disciplines and techniques. Intended for scientists and engineers with some knowledge of Russian. A work of exceptional quality, carefully compiled and edited, and well printed.

254 Clark, George L., and Hawley, Gassner G., eds. Encyclopedia of chemistry. 2d ed. Reinhold, 1966. 1144p. $25.

This unique one-volume encyclopedia covers the field of chemical knowledge with a surprising degree of depth. Approximately one third of the articles are new to this edition, and most of the remainder have been thoroughly revised. However, articles dealing with famous chemists and institutions have been reluctantly dropped. A 30-page index with about 5000 entries facilitates location of information not readily found in the alphabetized contents.

255 Condensed chemical dictionary. Compl. rev. and enl. by Arthur and Elizabeth Rose. 7th ed. Reinhold, 1966. 1044p. $20.

Defines principal terms and concisely describes commercial and trademarked chemical products. Terminology reflecting the advances in thermonuclear phenomena has been added. Also serves as an excellent source of information about official pharmaceuticals and drugs.

256 Condon, Edward Uhler, and Odishaw, Hugh, eds. Handbook of physics. 2d ed. McGraw-Hill, 1967. Unpaged. $32.50.
A brave attempt to condense the whole of physics into one volume. Emphasizes theory and omits experimental methods and data. Bibliography for each of the articles.

257 Handbook of chemistry and physics: a ready-reference book of chemical and physical data. Edited by R. C. Weast. Chemical Rubber Co. Annual. $17.50.
A compilation of essential tables of physical and chemical properties of elements and compounds.

258 Mellon, Melvin Guy. Chemical publications: their use and nature. McGraw-Hill, 1965. 4th ed. 324p. $9.50.
A well-organized undergraduate work describing the various types of literature. Devotes a section to library problems for the student.

259 Merck index of chemicals and drugs. 7th ed. Edited by Paul G. Stecher. Merck, 1960. 1642p. $12.
Approximately 10,000 chemical substances are described, and properties such as boiling point, color, etc., are given. There are, in addition, some 30,000 proprietary and trade names cross-indexed. Medical and other uses are also provided.

Geology

260 Challinor, John. A dictionary of geology. 2d ed. Oxford Univ. Pr., 1964. 289p. $5.
A more than adequate work which defines terms and examines meanings and concepts. Selected quotations and references support most entries.

261 Pough, Frederick H. A field guide to rocks and minerals. 3d ed. Houghton, 1960. 349p. $4.95.

An excellent handbook for identification purposes. Photographs of rocks and minerals are accompanied by a diagrammatic sketch of the crystal shape of the mineral and a description of its physical properties, composition, identification tests, and distinguishing characteristics.

262 Ransom, Jay E. Fossils in America; their nature, origin, identification, and classification and a range guide to collecting sites. Harper, 1964. 402p. $8.95.

Elementary background materials on fossil collection and identification, field geology, and map reading are outlined. More than half the book is an alphabetical directory of fossil-hunting spots; places are arranged by state, county, township, and sections providing species or genera of collectible fossils. For fossil hunters and beginning paleontologists. Lists libraries and mineral museums in the United States.

263 Shipley, Robert Morrill, assisted by Beckley, Anna McConnell, [and others]. Dictionary of gems and gemology including ornamental, decorative, and curio stones; a glossary of over 4000 English and foreign words, terms, and abbreviations which may be encountered in English literature on the gem, jewelry, or art trades. 5th ed. Gemological Institute of America, 1951. 261p. $5.50.

Includes historical matter and gives pronunciation. Reference is occasionally made to authority supplying specific information, with entry also under the authority.

264 Sinkankas, John. Mineralogy; a first course. Van Nostrand, 1966. 587p. $8.95.

Formerly called *Mineralogy for Amateurs,* this is for the nonbeginning amateur. Covers more than 250 minerals with full descriptions and information on where to look for specimens. Emphasis on drawings and photographs. Technical language has been kept at a minimum. Includes an excellent, highly selective bibliography.

265 Webster, R. A. Gems, their sources, descriptions, and identi-

fication. Butterworth & Co. (Shoe String), 1962. 2v. $32.

A landmark work on precious stones by a gemologist who is able to describe both the materials and the instruments by which they are studied. Volume 1 includes gem material descriptions; Volume 2 deals with technical aspects and the various methods of gem identification. Color plates and extensive identification tables are included.

Mathematics

266 Barlow, Peter. Barlow's Tables of squares, cubes, square roots, cube roots and reciprocals of all integer numbers up to 12,500. Edited by L. J. Comrie. 4th ed. Chemical Pub. Co., 1962 (c1941). 258p. $4.95.

Highly utilitarian compilations, valuable to laymen and scientists alike. Exceptionally accurate.

267 James, Glenn, and James, Robert Clarke, eds. Mathematics dictionary. Multilingual edition. Van Nostrand, 1959. 546p. $16.50. (New ed. in prep.)

A correlated condensation of mathematical concepts designed to serve the needs of both students and scholars. Format suitable for highspeed reference work.

268 Jones, Stacy W. Weights and measures. Public Affairs Press, 1963. 141p. $3.50.

Dictionary of weights and measures for the layman and student. Defines familiar units and standards as well as those of the newer technologies, including history of the units and authority for their accuracy. Appendix contains tables of equivalents for lengths, areas or surfaces, capacities or volumes, weights or masses, and kitchen units.

269 Naft, Stephen. International conversion tables. Expanded and rev. by Ralph DeSola. Duell, 1961. 372p. $7.95.

Accurate and handy ready-reference source for persons in international commerce, science, and management occupations.

Authority is U.S. Bureau of Standards to the extent that United States standards are available.

270 Zimmerman, Oswald Theodore, and Lavine, Irvin. Industrial Research Services' Conversion factors and tables. 3d ed. Industrial Res. Ser., 1961. 680p. $7.50.

An indispensable reference tool whose latest edition has been updated and expanded to include new standards and new values for pertinent physical constants. Has a section on foreign units and monetary equivalents.

Zoology

271 American Kennel Club. Complete dog book. Rev. ed. Doubleday, 1961. 524p. $4.95.

Covers the care, feeding, and handling of purebred dogs, plus a wealth of other information.

272 Burt, William Henry, and Grossenheider, R. P. A field guide to the mammals. 2d ed. rev. and enl. Houghton, 1964. 284p. $4.95

Covers North American mammals and drawings, photographs, and brief notes on recognition, habitat, habits, young, range, and economic status. Skulls are also covered. Subspecies have been omitted. Includes bibliography. Indexed.

273 Chu, Hung-fu. How to know the immature insects. Edited by Harry E. Jaques. W. C. Brown, 1949. 234p. $3.50; paper $2.75.

An excellent guide. Drawings are accurate, and the text frequently includes notes indicating useful or harmful qualities.

274 Conant, Roger. A field guide to reptiles and amphibians of the United States and Canada east of the 100th meridian. Houghton, 1958. 366p. $4.95.

The identification, care, and collecting of Eastern reptiles and amphibians is covered. Illustrations are excellent.

275 Miller, William Christopher, and West, Geoffrey P. Encyclopedia of animal care. 7th ed. Williams & Wilkins, 1964. 1017p. $9.

Earlier editions were published under the title *Black's Veterinary Dictionary*. Covers both domestic and wild animals. Well illustrated.

276 Morris, Percy A. A field guide to the shells of our Atlantic and Gulf coasts. Rev. and enl. ed. Houghton, 1951. 236p. $4.95.

This guide and its companion volume, *A Field Guide to Shells of the Pacific Coast and Hawaii,* cover the more common shellfish found on North American and Hawaiian beaches. Well illustrated with photographs. Text lists likely areas where the shells can be found and provides information on how to handle the specimens collected.

277 Murie, Olaus Johan. A field guide to animal tracks. Houghton, 1954. 400p. $4.95.

Every mammal for which tracks have been obtained in North and Central America is included. Each animal's typical habits and peculiarities are discussed in the text. Birds and reptiles are covered briefly.

278 Pennak, Robert William. Collegiate dictionary of zoology. Ronald, 1964. 583p. $8.50.

A useful dictionary containing about 19,000 definitions of zoological terms commonly not explained in zoological texts. Proper names are included.

279 Peterson, Roger Tory. A field guide to the birds; giving field marks of all species found east of the Rockies. 2d rev. and enl. ed. Houghton, 1947. 290p. $4.95.

A well-illustrated guide covering 702 forms of birds found east of the 100th meridian. Subspecies are listed only if field markings are obvious. Only the Eastern North American range is given for the birds covered. Libraries in the West will want

A Field Guide to Western Birds. Libraries in border states will want both. Sponsored by the National Audubon Society.

280 ———A field guide to western birds; field marks of all species found in North America west of the 100th meridian with a section on the birds of the Hawaiian Islands. 2d rev. and enl. ed. Houghton, 1961. 366p. $4.95.

Companion volume to Peterson's *A Field Guide to the Birds.* See annotation above.

281 Swain, Ralph B. Insect guide; orders and major families of North American insects. Doubleday, 1948. 261p. $4.95.

Text includes notes on the adult forms, the young, and the importance to man of each. Illustrations are centered in the text and are adequate.

► In addition, libraries may want to have books on cats, tropical fish, pet birds, etc., depending on local interest.

Applied Science

Agriculture

282 U.S. Department of Agriculture. Yearbook of agriculture. Govt. Print. Off., 1936– . Annual. About $4.

Each yearbook is devoted to a specific subject, e.g., *Farmer's World* (1964) and *Consumers All* (1965). Some of these, because of the subject, do not belong on the reference shelf, but others—such as those on *Trees* (1949), *Water* (1955), *Food* (1959), and *Seeds* (1961)—will be highly useful for a long time to come.

Electronics

283 Hahn, Steven. Hi-fi handbook: a guide to monaural and stereophonic reproduction. 2d ed. rev. by William J. Kendall. Crowell, 1962. 216p. $4.95.

Highly practical reference work. A great deal of nontechnical information on understanding, evaluating, purchasing, and installing high-fidelity equipment. To update price and model information, reference should be made to *High Fidelity* or similar magazines.

284 Hicks, David E. Citizen's band radio handbook. 2d ed. Sams, 1964. 192p. $3.50.

The increasing number of people using the citizen's radio service makes this a highly useful book. Simple language, comprehensive, well illustrated.

285 Radio amateur's handbook. Am. Radio, 1926– . Annual. $6.

The bible for "hams," this volume contains a wealth of information on equipment, operations, and regulations. It is also valuable for the amateur who wishes to obtain a license. Superseded editions should be put in the circulating collection.

286 Stetka, Frank, and Brandon, Merwin M. NFPA handbook of the National electrical code. McGraw-Hill, 1966. $12.75.

Some of this material appeared in the 1965 *National Electrical Code Handbook,* edited by Arthur L. Abbott. Topics covered: wiring design, methods, and materials; equipment; special occupancies and conditions; communication systems. For local regulations, copies of the municipal building code should also be available.

287 Susskind, Charles, ed. Encyclopedia of electronics. Reinhold, 1962. 974p. $25.

Contains more than 500 articles written by specialists. Somewhat advanced but should be comprehensible to the informed general reader. Well indexed and cross referenced.

Engineering and Mechanics

288 Brady, George S. Materials handbook; an encyclopedia for purchasing agents, engineers, executives, and foremen. 9th ed. McGraw-Hill, 1963. 968p. $17.50.

A long-established cyclopedic work of technical and trade information on approximately 12,000 materials of commercial importance, ranging from brick to walrus hide. Descriptive essays vary greatly in length; they include source, physical properties, and uses. Trade names are often mentioned. Includes a short but important section on economic geography.

289 Crispin, Frederic Swing. Dictionary of technical terms; containing definitions of commonly used expressions in aeronautics, architecture, woodworking and building trades, electrical and metalworking trades, printing, chemistry, plastics, etc. 10th ed. rev. Bruce, 1964. 455p. $5.50.

Intended for students, draftsmen, technicians, mechanics, and others engaged in practical technical work. About 10,000 terms defined briefly, i.e., in one or two lines. Includes pronunciation.

290 Glenn, H. T. Glenn's New auto repair manual. Chilton, 1966. 1392p. $9.95.

See note under *Motor Service Magazine* below.

291 Jones, Franklin Day, and Schubert, Paul B., eds. Engineering encyclopedia. 3d ed. Industrial Press, 1963. 1431p. $15.

The best one-volume work on engineering for the layman as well as for the practicing mechanic and technician.

292 LeGrand, Rupert, ed. New American machinist's handbook. Based on . . . American machinist's handbook. Edited by Fred H. Colvin and Frank A. Stanley. McGraw-Hill, 1955. Unpaged. $15.

A wealth of information on all aspects of metalworking. 45 sections, each separately paged, each devoted to a specific aspect such as filing, grinding, fasteners, metal forming, or tool engineering.

293 McLaughlin, Charles, ed. Space age dictionary. 2d ed. Van Nostrand, 1963. 236p. $7.95.

Brief entries. Several good tabular lists of data, such as space flights, launchings, satellites in orbit. Will be most useful for definitions of terms.

294 Motor Service Magazine. Motor Service's New automotive encyclopedia. Edited by William K. Toboldt and Jud Purvis. Goodheart-Willcox, 1964. Unpaged. $8.95.

Libraries have a difficult time keeping the automotive books, yet they are essential reference tools. Both *Glenn* and this one are revised frequently and contain information on cars manufactured within the previous ten to fifteen years. Old editions, if they have not disappeared, should be kept.

Health and Medicine

295 Clark, Randolph Lee, and Cumley, Russell W., eds. Book of health. 2d ed. Van Nostrand, 1962. 888p. $17.50.

Clear, concise information for the layman on human diseases, the structure of the organs involved, and the healing treatment. 255 contributors. Highly readable. Well illustrated and indexed.

296 Diehl, Harold S. Healthful living; a textbook of personal and community living. 7th ed. McGraw-Hill, 1964. 691p. $10.50.

An outstanding textbook on health education which is most useful as a reference tool. Among other topics, includes chapters on nutrition and growth, personal hygiene, mental health, and control of communicable diseases in man. Glossary and index.

297 Dorland's Illustrated medical dictionary. 24th ed. Saunders, 1965. 1724p. $13.

Frequently revised, this is the most widely used and most reliable of the medical dictionaries. Contains, along with definitions of current usage, lists of valuable information under such headings as "tests," "diseases," and "signs." If use warrants the purchase of more than one medical dictionary, *Blakiston's New Gould Medical Dictionary* (2d ed., McGraw-Hill, 1956) and

Thomas Lathrop Stedman's *Medical Dictionary* (21st ed. comp. rev., Williams & Wilkins, 1966) are also recommended.

298 Drugs in current use. Edited by Walter Modell. Springer Pub., 1955– . Annual. Paper $2.75.

An alphabetical list of drugs currently used in clinical medicine. Gives characteristics, properties, uses, mode of action, and precautions. Useful to supplement Merck between editions.

299 Dublin, Louis Israel. Factbook on man; from birth to death. 2d ed. Macmillan, 1965. 465p. $7.95.

Using the question-and-answer technique, this book provides a wealth of information and statistics in the field of human biology. Includes a list of selected references. Indexed.

300 Encyclopedia of child care and guidance. Edited by Sidonie Matsner Gruenberg. Rev. ed. Doubleday, 1963. 1016p. $8.50. (New ed. in prep.)

In two parts: The first is an alphabetical arrangement by topic and will be of interest to parents and laymen in general. Contains a list of agencies and organizations and an annotated bibliography. The second part, "Basic Aspects of Child Development," is a series of articles by specialists which will be used by educators, psychologists, and counselors. Comprehensive, modern, and authoritative.

301 Gray, Henry. Anatomy of the human body. 28th ed. Lea & Febiger, 1966. 1448p. $22.50.

The classic text in the field and a standard reference tool. More than 1000 illustrations, nearly half in color, plus one of the most comprehensive and detailed indexes to be found in any reference book. Revised every few years.

302 Hammond (C. S.) and Company, Inc. Human anatomy atlas. Hammond, 1961. Unpaged. Paper $1.

32 full-color illustrations. Useful as an adjunct to Gray (above).

303 Hinsie, Leland Earl, and Campbell, Robert Jean. Psychiatric dictionary. 3d ed. Oxford Univ. Pr., 1960. 788p. $17.50.

Somewhat advanced in level of definition but useful as a supplement to medical and general dictionaries. Includes psychosomatic medicine, adolescent and geriatric psychology, and drugs used in psychotherapy and psychoanalysis. Gives pronunciation, cites quotations showing use of term, and references.

304 Red Cross. U.S. American National Red Cross. First aid text book. 4th ed. rev. Doubleday, 1957. 241p. $1; paper $.75.

Authoritative, concise, simply explained. Well illustrated. Latest edition only should be kept because of recent changes in artificial respiration, among other topics.

305 Sax, Newton Irving, and others, eds. Dangerous properties of industrial materials. 2d ed. Reinhold, 1963. 1343p. $25.

Contains general information on toxicology, air pollution, radiation, etc., as well as on storage and handling of hazardous materials. Main part of the work is an alphabetic arrangement of substances giving for each: general information, hazard analysis, countermeasures, with cross reference to general information section for storage and handling and for shipping regulations.

House and Garden

306 Farmer, Fannie M. Fannie Farmer cook book. 11th rev. ed. by Wilma L. Perkins. Little, 1965. 624p. $6.95.

A classic that has served the American housewife for many years. Later editions have been thoroughly revised to include modern recipes and methods.

307 Montagné, Prosper. Larousse gastronomique; the encyclopedia of food, wine, and cookery. Edited by Charlotte Turgeon and Nina Froud. Crown, 1961. 1101p. $20.

Recipes and foods from all countries arranged in encyclopedic form. Illustrations, a few in color. Gastronomic maps of provinces of France. Index and bibliography in French, but text is in English.

308 Rombauer, Irma Von Starkloff, and Becker, Marion Rombauer. The joy of cooking. Rev. and enl. ed. Bobbs, 1962. 852p. $6.50.

A basic cookbook, somewhat more European in tone than *The Fannie Farmer Cook Book,* but excellent in the quality of its recipes and in its discussion of the preparation and serving of food.

309 Gladstone, Bernard. New York Times complete manual of home repair. Macmillan, 1966. 438p. $7.95.

Taken from the author's very popular column in the *New York Times,* this is an excellent collection of practical information on how to do it and how not to do it for the home handyman (and the not-so-handy). Illustrated.

310 Moore, Alma Chesnut. How to clean everything; an encyclopedia of what to use and how to use it. Rev. ed. Simon & Schuster, 1961. 203p. $3.95.

An excellent handbook to use in answering telephone reference questions.

311 Taylor, Norman, ed. Encyclopedia of gardening: horticulture and landscape design. 4th ed. rev. and enl. Houghton, 1961. 1329p. $9.95.

Contains information on more than 9000 species of American and Canadian plants. Gives information on soils, climate, growing methods, and plant diseases in general, as well as specific information on raising individual species.

Plastics and Textiles

312 Linton, George Edward. Modern textile dictionary. Rev. and enl. ed. Meredith, 1963. 1077p. $18.50.

More than 10,000 terms relating to fabrics, their manufacture, description, and uses.

313 Simonds, Herbert Rumsey, and Church, James Marion. A concise guide to plastics. 2d ed. Reinhold, 1963. 392p. $12.

The best one-volume reference work on plastics designed for the non-specialist. Information on uses, properties, costs, and sources of a multitude of plastic materials. Includes a list of manufacturers and their addresses, various divisions, trade names of their product, and their financial statement. In addition to a general index there is an index to trade names.

9
Art

General Works

Indexes

314 Art index 1929–   ; a cumulative author and subject index to a selected list of fine arts periodicals and museum bulletins. Wilson. Quarterly with cumulations. Service basis.

Indexes 120 periodicals. Basic tool for libraries serving art-conscious communities and subscribing to art periodicals.

315 Vance, Lucille E., and Tracy, Esther M. Illustration index. 2d ed. Scarecrow, 1966. 527p. $12.

Revised and expanded subject index to 12 popular periodicals and a few books, 1950–June, 1963. Ready-reference source for photographs, charts, drawings, and paintings.

Dictionaries and Encyclopedias

316 Adeline, Jules. Adeline art dictionary, including terms in architecture, heraldry, and archeology. Trans. from the French. With a supplement of new terms by Hugo G. Beigel. Ungar, 1966. 459p. $9.50.

Includes ancient and modern terms, both technical and in general use. "A large amount of information has been incorporated from F. W. Fairholt's *Dictionary of Terms in Art.*"

317 Encyclopaedia of the arts. Consulting ed., Herbert Read. Meredith, 1966. 966p. $35.

Precise and specific information relating to the arts of the Western world. Includes entries for individuals and for particular works of art, and articles on historical movements in the arts and on materials and techniques. Well illustrated. Classified and alphabetical bibliographies.

318 Murray, Peter, and Murray, Linda. Dictionary of art and artists. Praeger, 1966 (c1959). 464p. $14.95.

Includes brief selected biographies chiefly of Western European artists, from about 1300 to the present day, and art terms not adequately defined in most general dictionaries. Illustrations make up the latter half of the volume. Useful for ready reference.

319 Praeger picture encyclopedia of art; a comprehensive survey of painting, sculpture, architecture and crafts, their methods, styles and technical terms, from the earliest times to the present day. Praeger, 1958. 584p. $13.95.

Useful source book for art through the ages, covering the important periods in six parts, with "Art—Its Nature, Forms and History" and "Art outside Europe" as introduction and finale. Encyclopedic material at end of each section. Comprehensive index. Well illustrated, many illustrations in color.

320 Whittick, Arnold. Symbols, signs and their meaning. Branford, 1960. 408p. $12.95.

Symbols in general, "traditional and familiar, their origins, meaning and history" in encyclopedic form. Includes bibliography for each symbol. Also contains section on "symbolism in its precise and applied forms, and its practical uses." Well illustrated and indexed.

Directories

321 American art directory, 1898–   . Bowker. Triennial since 1952. $22.50.

Originally *American Art Annual*. Lists museums, art organ-

izations, art departments in universities and colleges, art magazines, scholarships and fellowships, traveling exhibitions, and
other miscellaneous information of interest to the art world.
Mainly on United States, but does include Canada and a list of
major museums abroad.

History

322 Cheney, Sheldon. A new world history of art. Compl. rev.
ed. with additional text. Viking, 1956. 676p. $10.95.
General treatment of the visual arts. Includes descriptive
bibliography. Location of original is noted under each illustration.

323 Gardner, Helen. Art through the ages. 4th ed. rev. under
the editorship of Sumner M. Crosby. Harcourt, 1959. 840p.
$13.25.
Art history surveyed from early to modern times, for the
student and general reader. Includes a glossary, a comprehensive index, and bibliographies.

324 Janson, Horst Woldemar, and Janson, Dora Jane. History
of art; a survey of the major visual arts from the dawn of history to the present day. Abrams, 1962. 572p. $18.50.
Can be used as a textbook or as a scholarly reference source.
Includes bibliography and index. Illustrated.

325 Larkin, Oliver W. Art and life in America. Rev. and enl.
ed. Holt, 1960. 559p. $17.25.
Covers the field from 1600 to 1960. Earlier edition awarded
the Pulitzer Prize in history. Includes bibliography and is well
indexed.

326 Robb, David Methany, and Garrison, Jessie James. Art in
the Western world. 4th ed. Harper, 1963. 782p. $9.95.
A revision of a standard text with new illustrations and indexes. Includes a glossary, bibliography, and a chronological
table.

327 Spaeth, Eloise. American art museums and galleries; an introduction to looking. Harper, 1960. 282p. $5.95.

A description and history of the best pieces in each museum and the characteristics of each gallery. Grouped geographically. Omits college, university, and the largest metropolitan museums. Last section lists approximately 125 key galleries in the United States, giving character, specialties, and price ranges.

Architecture

328 American architects directory. Edited by George S. Koyl. 2d ed. Published under the sponsorship of American Institute of Architects. Bowker, 1962. 919p. $25.

Includes all members of the Institute, except where omission has been requested, and other eligible architects. Omits most biographical facts not relevant to architectural training and practice. Arranged alphabetically with geographical index of architects.

329 Briggs, Martin Shaw. Everyman's concise encyclopedia of architecture. Dutton, 1960 (c1959). 372p. $5.50.

Includes definitions, brief biographies, and short articles on the history of architecture. References given for more important subjects. Line drawings and a section of 32 plates are included.

330 Dictionary of architectural abbreviations, signs, and symbols. Ed., David D. Polon. Managing ed., Herbert W. Reich. Project director, Marjorie B. Whilty. Associate ed., William H. Walker. Golden Pr., 1966 (c1965). (The Odyssey scientific library) 595p. $20.

An attempt is made to identify and standardize signs, abbreviations, and symbols as they are used in architectural texts and on the drawing board. Architectural degrees and associations are included.

331 Fletcher, *Sir* Banister Flight. A history of architecture on

the comparative method. 17th ed. rev. by R. A. Cordingley. Scribner, 1961. 1366p. $17.95.

The first major revision of a standard reference work; profusely illustrated. Includes chapter bibliographies, a list of general reference books, and a glossary of architectural terms.

332 Hamlin, Talbot Faulkner. Architecture through the ages. Rev. ed. Putnam, 1953. 684p. $9.50.

Originally published in 1940. A good one-volume history. Well illustrated.

333 Jones, Cranston. Architecture today and tomorrow. McGraw-Hill, 1961. 243p. $17.50.

Analysis of twentieth-century architecture by an examination of the works and words of the best-known architects. Well illustrated.

334 Kimball, Sidney Fiske, and Edgell, George Harold. A history of architecture. Harper (c1918). 621p. $7.50.

A useful handbook, including Bibliographical Note and a chronological list of architectural examples at the end of each chapter. Glossary. Illustrated.

335 Ware, Dora, and Beatty, Betty. A short dictionary of architecture, including some common building terms. With an introduction on The study of architecture, by John Gloag. [3d ed. rev. and enl.] Hillary House, [1953]. 136p. $3.

The standard dictionary in its field for commonly-used terms in classical and current architecture.

Sculpture and the Plastic Arts

Sculpture

336 New York. Metropolitan Museum of Art. American sculpture; a catalogue of the collection of the Metropolitan Museum of Art, by Albert Ten Eyck Gardner. Distributed by New York Graphic, 1965. 192p. $7.50.

Brief biographies of the American sculptors in the collection, with descriptive and informative notes on one or more works of each. Arranged chronologically. Good index. Illustrated.

Numismatics

337 Red book of United States coins; a guidebook. Whitman. Annual. $2 (1967).

Editor, 1946 to date: R. S. Yeoman. Catalog and price list of coins from A.D. 1616 to date, including early tokens, commemorative issues, proofs, etc., as well as a brief history of American coinage. Illustrated.

338 Reinfeld, Fred. A catalogue of the world's most popular coins. Expanded ed. rev. by Burton Hobson. Doubleday, 1967. 288p. $7.50.

Modern and ancient coins and their values. Arranged by country with historical notes about each. Many illustrations. Includes those coins most sought by collectors and most likely to increase in value.

339 Slabaugh, Arlie R. United States commemorative coins; the drama of America as told by our coins. Whitman, 1963. 144p. $2.

Historical and related information provides material to interest the general reader, as well as coin collectors. Illustrated.

Ceramics

340 Chaffers, William. Marks and monograms on European and Oriental pottery and porcelain. The British section edited by Geoffrey A. Godden. The European and Oriental sections edited by Frederick Litchfield and R. L. Hobson. 15th rev. ed. Borden, 1965. 2v. $19.95.

Usually considered the standard work on pottery marks. Includes bibliography.

341 Cushion, J. P., and Honey, William Bowyer. Handbook of pottery and porcelain marks. 3d ed. Faber, 1956. 476p. $7.65.

Includes many nineteenth- and twentieth-century marks, as well as earlier ones. Arranged by country; includes Europe, China, and Japan. Good index.

342 Eberlein, Harold Donaldson, and Ramsdell, Roger Wearne. Practical book of chinaware. Rev. ed. Lippincott, 1948. 320p. $10.

Answers questions on the less-rare types of china which are likely to be considered treasures by average collectors. Covers the china of all countries. Includes bibliography. 120 plates, a few in color.

Art Metalwork

343 Wyler, Seymour B. Book of old silver, English, American, foreign. With all available hallmarks, including Sheffield plate marks. Crown, 1937. 447p. $5.

A comprehensive, indexed table of hallmarks facilitates identification of silver. Contains chapters on various types of silver articles, e.g., tea and condiment sets, flat and table ware, boxes, etc.

Decorative Arts and Design

344 Aronson, Joseph. Encyclopedia of furniture. 3d ed. comp. rev. Crown, 1965. 484p. $7.95.

Easy access to brief information, illustrated with photographs and line cuts. Glossary of designers and craftsmen; bibliography.

345 Bernasconi, John R. Collectors' glossary of antiques and fine arts. Transatlantic Arts, 1966. 587p. $11.50.

Of interest to the collector and to those in the antiques business, also to libraries because of the amount of useful information. An excellent source, also, for symbols in classical, religious, heraldic, and Chinese arts.

346 Boger, Louise Ade, and Boger, H. Batterson. Dictionary of antiques and the decorative arts; a book of reference for glass, furniture, ceramics, silver, periods, styles, technical terms, etc. 2d ed. Scribner, 1967. 662p. $17.50.

Alphabetically arranged entries cover America, Europe, and the Orient. Brief biographies and brief period histories. Revised ed. contains supplement defining 700 new terms and brief biographies.

347 Comstock, Helen, ed. Concise encyclopedia of American antiques. Hawthorn, 1965. 848p. $12.50.

Originally issued in two volumes in 1958. Does not include material reprinted from the *Connoisseur's Concise Encyclopedia of Antiques,* 1955–61 (Volumes 1 and 5 now out of print), but is a comprehensive work of new material written by authorities in their various fields, including some hard to find in antique books: marine prints, folk art, firearms, theater and circus playbills, etc. Includes bibliographies.

348 Gloag, John. A short dictionary of furniture; containing 1767 terms used in Britain and America. Holt, 1965. 565p. $7.95.

Description of furniture and accessories from A.D. 1100 to the mid-seventeenth century. Includes a list of furniture makers, an outline of the development of furniture, and a bibliography.

349 Hayward, Helena, ed. Connoisseur's handbook of antique collecting; a dictionary of furniture, silver, ceramics, glass, fine art, etc. Hawthorn, 1960. 320p. $5.95.

A useful work, which may be most valuable for definition of terms. Includes historical outlines and a select bibliography.

350 Kamm, Minnie Elizabeth (Watson). Kamm Wood encyclopedia of antique pattern glass. Serry Wood, pseud., ed. Century House, 1961. 2v. $22.

Arranged by names of patterns. Describes collectable standard pattern glass from the nineteenth century to about 1915.

351 Macdonald-Taylor, Margaret Stephens. A dictionary of

marks, metalwork, furniture, ceramics, the identification handbook for antique collectors. Hawthorn, 1962. 318p. $5.95.

A guide to the identification of American, English, and Continental antiques. Section on ceramics lists Japanese date marks and Chinese reign marks. Includes bibliography.

352 McKearin, George Skinner, and McKearin, Helen. American glass. 2,000 photos, 1,000 drawings by James L. McCreery. Crown, 1948. 634p. $12.95.

History of the development of glassmaking in America and guide for the identification of American glass.

353 Meyer, Franz Sales. Handbook of ornament; a grammar of art, industrial and architectural designing in all its branches for practical as well as theoretical use. Dover, 1957. 548p. Paper $2.75.

A republication of a standard handbook. Well illustrated and indexed.

354 Miller, Edgar George. American antique furniture, a book for amateurs. Dover, 1966. 2v. Paper $3.75 each.

Entries and illustrations are arranged by type, and show changes of style in successive periods. Stresses important features for those who wish to live with antiques. Volume 2 lists museums and collections in New England open to the public.

355 Pegler, Martin. Dictionary of interior design. Crown, 1966. 500p. $7.50.

Concise definitions covering elements of interior design, old and new, from horsehair to furniture. Small illustrations with text. Includes brief biographies about individuals in design and associated fields.

356 Shull, Thelma. Victorian antiques. Tuttle, 1963. 421p. $12.75.

A guide to the objects of art, utilitarian or otherwise, made during the Victorian period and to their use, such as "language of the fan." Includes bibliography and illustrations.

357 Speltz, Alexander. The styles of ornament. 2d ed. Dover, 1960. 647p. Paper $3.

Aims to represent "the entire range of ornament in all its different styles from pre-historic times 'till the middle of the 19th century." A republication of David O'Conor's translation from the second German edition. Includes bibliography.

358 Zielinski, Stanislaw A. Encyclopaedia of hand-weaving. Funk, 1959. 190p. $8.50.

Excellent for definition and derivation of terms, variations in meaning in Britain and the United States, and general information about weaving. Sketch drawings, pattern drafts, and photographs illustrate text.

Painting

359 Encyclopedia of painting; painters and painting of the world from prehistoric times to the present day. Bernard S. Myers, ed. Crown, 1955. 511p. $12.95.

Definitions of technical terms, histories of movements in painting, lengthy articles on painting in various countries, and biographies of great painters are arranged in dictionary form. Illustrations, many in color, accompany text.

360 Haftmann, Werner. Painting in the twentieth century. Rev. ed. Praeger, 1965. 2v. $17.50; paper $3.95. Picture ed. paper $5.95.

A definitive survey and comprehensive analysis of twentieth-century painting. Biographical section contains more than 400 listings.

361 Mayer, Ralph. Artist's handbook of material and techniques. Rev. ed. Viking, 1957. 721p. $6.95.

Excellent guide for both amateur and professional. With this in the reference collection, both Doerner, *Materials of the Artist,* and Taubes, *Guide to Traditional and Modern Painting Methods,* can be put into the circulating collection.

362 Monro, Isabel S., and Monro, Kate M. Index to reproductions of American paintings and first supplement. Wilson, 1948, 1964. 731p., 480p. $12.50; $15.

An index to reproductions in 520 books and more than 300 exhibition catalogs by name of artist, title of painting, and subject. Locations of the original paintings are given when known.

363 ————Index to reproductions of European paintings. Wilson, 1956. 668p. $12.50.

A guide to pictures by European artists that are reproduced in 328 books. Paintings are entered under name of artist, title of painting, and, in many cases, subject. Locations of original paintings are noted whenever known.

364 New York Graphic Society. Fine art reproductions of old and modern masters; a comprehensive illustrated catalog through the ages. The Society, 1965. 540p. $25.

Primarily intended as a catalog of prints distributed by the New York Graphic Society, this volume offers an extensive pictorial history of painting through the ages. Dates of artists and of painting, and size and price of prints are noted under each illustration.

365 Robb, David M. Harper history of painting: the Occidental tradition. Harper, 1951. 1006p. $11.75.

Covers preclassic to contemporary painting and painters. Glossary and selected bibliography included.

366 United Nations Educational, Scientific and Cultural Organization. Catalogue of color reproductions of paintings prior to 1860. 7th ed. UNESCO or Int. Pub. Ser., 1964. 379p. $6.

367 ————Catalogue of color reproductions, 1860–1965. 8th ed. UNESCO or Int. Pub. Ser., 1966. 561p. $7.

Small black-and-white reproductions, together with size, price, and publisher, provide the information necessary for purchasing color reproductions available from various publishers.

Photography

368 Focal encyclopedia of photography. Fully rev. ed. Focal Press, 1965. 2v. $39.

Technologies, subjects, and terminologies, many new to photography during the past decade, are covered in this library of photographic science, industrial photography, cinematography, portraiture, equipment, history, statistics, biographies, and activities in foreign countries. Beware of the single-volume desk edition, 1960, which is a condensation of the 1956 edition and therefore largely obsolete.

Costume

369 Davenport, Millia. Book of costume. Crown, 1948 (reprinted 1962). 958p. $12.95.

Originally in two volumes, but now available in this one-volume edition. Basic information ends in 1867. Includes costumes of the Orient, Europe, and America, as well as ecclesiastical vestments, habits of monastic orders, and the dress of the Roman army. Arranged chronologically. Many excellent illustrations, with location of original for a majority. Detailed index.

370 Evans, Mary. Costume through the ages. 3d ed. Lippincott, 1950. 360p. $6.95.

An excellent introduction to the subject. Many illustrations. Bibliographies for each chapter and a general bibliography. Index.

371 Monro, Isabel Stevenson, and Monro, Kate M., eds. Costume index supplement; a subject index to plates and to illustrated text. Wilson, 1957. 210p. $6.

Indexes the plates and pictures in 347 books. Covers all historical periods. Almost all nationalities and classes of society are included. Annotations are given for the books which have been indexed. The 1937 edition of *Costume Index,* to which this volume is a supplement, is out of print (1967).

372 Payne, Blanche. History of costume: from the ancient Egyptians to the twentieth century. Harper, 1965. 607p. $13.50.

Fully illustrated with photographs of paintings, statuary, and actual costumes, as well as with line drawings. Accessories are included, and 50 pages of draft patterns. Concluding date is 1900. Bibliography; detailed index.

373 Picken, Mary B. Fashion dictionary; fabric, sewing and dress as expressed in the language of fashion. Funk, 1956. 397p. $10.

A useful reference book for costume, as well as for textiles and clothing. Includes more than 10,000 terms and names associated with clothing, fashions, and fabrics. Gives pronunciation. Many illustrations. Based on the author's *The Language of Fashion*.

374 Wilcox, Ruth Turner. Five centuries of American costume. Scribner, 1963. 207p. $6.50.

The dress of American men, women, and children, from the Vikings, Eskimos, and early settlers to 1960. Arranged chronologically. Clear line drawings illustrate the text. Bibliography. Lacks an index.

375 ———Mode in costume. 2d ed. Scribner, 1958. 463p. $8.95.

Covers costume from the Egyptians of 3000 B.C. to 1958. Accessories are included. Clear drawings. Bibliography but no index.

10
Music

376 Ewen, David. Encyclopedia of the opera. New enl. ed. Hill & Wang, 1963. 594p. $7.50.

Comprehensive source book on opera, including opera plots, history, characters in operas, premieres, biographies of performers, etc. Includes a separate pronunciation guide.

377 Feather, Leonard G. Encyclopedia of jazz. Rev. ed. Horizon, 1960. 527p. $15.

377a ———Encyclopedia of jazz in the sixties. Horizon, 1967. 312p. $15. 2v. boxed as a set. Horizon, 1967. $25.

Articles and polls on jazz, lists of jazz recordings, and brief biographies of all important jazz musicians. Includes calendar of musicians' birthdays, birthplaces of musicians by state and town, a list of jazz organizations, schools, and booking agencies, jazz record companies, etc.

378 Fuld, James J. Book of world-famous music; classical, popular, and folk. Crown, 1966. 564p. $12.50.

No other title really quite does what this book does. Several thousand songs, tunes, etc., are alphabetically indexed with the musical theme, and words, where applicable, are printed along with a brief history of the melody. Also gives brief biographical data on composers and lyricists.

379 Grove, *Sir* George. Grove's Dictionary of music and musicians. Edited by Eric Blom. 5th rev. ed. enl., 1954. Supplementary vol. to 5th ed. by Eric Blom and Enis Stevens. St. Martin's, 1961. 10v. $157.50; suppl. vol. sold separately $15.

Covers thoroughly all aspects of music, composers, and performers.

380 Haywood, Charles, ed. Folk songs of the world. Day, 1966. 320p. $10.95; lib. bdg. $9.95.

Contains the words (in original language and English translation) and music of 180 songs from 119 countries, with historical background and notes on each song. Includes discussion of musical culture of each area, a bibliography, a selected list of recordings, and an index of first lines.

381 Kobbé, Gustav. Kobbé's Complete opera book. Rev. ed. by *Lord* Harewood. Putnam, 1963. 1262p. $10.95.

Detailed description of each of the important operas with

musical quotations, plot synopses, characters, historical background, etc. Arranged by centuries subdivided into countries. Illustrated and indexed.

382 Lawless, Ray McKinley. Folksingers and folksongs in America. 2d ed. Duell, 1965. 750p. $10.

Detailed handbook of American folk music, including biographies, bibliographies, discography, information about folklore societies and folk festivals, etc. Reprint of 1960 edition with a supplement that updates earlier information.

383 Lubbock, Mark Hugh. Complete book of light opera. Appleton, 1962. 953p. $12.95.

Covers all the leading schools of operetta, opera bouffé, and musical comedy, both European and American, from 1850 to 1961. Gives title, composer, source, first production, characters, and plot of about 300 musicals. Arrangement is by five cities where one might see these musicals performed. Illustrated with photographs of composers and scenes from the musicals.

384 Sears, Minnie E., ed., assisted by Phyllis Crawford. Song index: an index to more than 12,000 songs. 648p. 1926. Song index supplement: an index to more than 7,000 songs. 366p. 1934. Shoe String, 1966. 2v. in 1. $27.50.

Lists titles, first lines, authors' names, and composers' names in a single alphabet with fullest information under title entry. Can be used to find words and music of a song, lists of songs by an author or composer, and poems which have been set to music.

385 Shapiro, Nat. Popular music, an annotated index of American popular songs. Adrian. v.1, 1950–59, 1964; v.2, 1940–49, 1965; v.3, 1960–64, 1966. $16 each.

A selected list of popular songs published 1940–64, arranged by year, then alphabetically by title; gives author, title, composer, publisher, and first or best selling record, indicating performer and record company. Introduction to Volume 3 indicates future volumes will cover the years before 1940. Each volume has a title index and a directory of music publishers.

386 Shaw, Martin Fallas, and Coleman, Henry. National anthems of the world. 2d ed. Pitman, 1963. 408p. $12.50.

Contains words and music of more than 130 national anthems of countries throughout the world, in the original languages as well as in English translations.

387 Thompson, Oscar, ed. International cyclopedia of music and musicians. Edited by Robert Sabin. 9th ed. Dodd, 1964. 2476p. $35.

Considering the size and price, this is the best one-volume work in the field. Appendix gives pronunciation of names and titles.

11
Theater and Dance

388 Balanchine, George. Balanchine's Complete stories of the great ballets. Doubleday, 1954. 615p. $6.95.

Detailed stories of more than 100 standard ballets, both classic and modern, in the repertories of American ballet companies. Includes sections on enjoyment, history, chronology, and children's ballets, careers in ballet, a glossary, annotated selection of ballet recordings, and a selected reading guide.

389 Dimmitt, Richard B. A title guide to the talkies. Scarecrow, 1965. 2v. $47.50.

Lists 16,000 feature-length motion pictures from October, 1927, until December, 1963, in alphabetical order. Gives title, company producing, date of release, and source from which adapted. A valuable source of information in connection with reruns on television.

390 Freedley, George, and Reeves, John A. A history of the theatre. Rev. with a supplementary section by George Freedley. Crown, 1956. 784p. $8.50.

Comprehensive world history of the theater from its beginnings in ancient Egypt to 1940, with supplement for period 1940–54, covering in chronological fashion the gradual evolution of drama as set against a background of political, religious, and social phenomena. Annotated bibliographies for main part of work and supplement. Illustrated.

391 Halliwell, Leslie. Filmgoer's companion. Rev. and expanded ed. Hill & Wang, 1967. 847p. $12.50.

A dictionary with brief entries for directors, actors, notable films, and related subjects, some of the last being essay length. Emphasis is on the British and American film scene since 1930.

392 Hartnoll, Phyllis, ed. Oxford companion to the theatre. 3d ed. Oxford Univ. Pr., 1967. 1088p. $15.

One-volume encyclopedia, covering all aspects of the theater in all countries and all periods up to the end of 1964, and to later dates for England, France, and the United States. Includes bibliography and illustrations.

393 International motion picture almanac. Eds., Charles S. Aaronson and associates. Quigley, 1929–   . Annual. $9.

Useful for quickly finding out when a motion picture was released. Lists producers, exhibitors, motion-picture companies, and other essential data of the motion-picture world.

394 International television almanac. Eds., Charles S. Aaronson and associates. Quigley, 1956–   . Annual. $9.

Does essentially for television what the *Motion Picture Almanac* does for motion pictures.

12
Games and Sports

395 Foster, Robert F. Foster's Complete Hoyle. Rev. ed. Lippincott, 1963. 697p. $5.95.

Subtitle: An encyclopedia of games, including all indoor
games played today, with suggestions for good play, illustrative
hands and all official laws to date, revised and enlarged with
complete laws of contract bridge and canasta.

396 Menke, Frank Grant. Encyclopedia of sports. 3d rev. ed.
Barnes, 1963. 1044p. $17.50.

Comprehensive historical, statistical, legendary, and instruc-
tional details of nearly 80 sports. Winners and their records
are given for each sport in chronological order.

397 Sports rules encyclopedia; the official rules for 38 sports and
games. Nat. Press, 1961. 563p. $7.95.

Contains official rules, with diagrams and charts, of 38 games
and sports that can be played at the high school and college
level. Gives name and address of organization furnishing rules
for each sport.

398 Turkin, Hy, and Thompson, S. C. Official encyclopedia of
baseball. 3d rev. ed. Barnes, 1963. 625p. $9.75.

Extensive source book of baseball facts and figures, including history, all-time records, rules, World Series data, etc. *The
World Almanac* is useful for keeping up to date on this subject.

13
Language

General Works

399 Mencken, Henry Louis. American language; an inquiry into the development of English in the United States. 4th ed. and the two supplements, abridged, with annotations and new material by Raven I. McDavid, Jr. 1st abridged ed. Knopf, 1963. 777p. $12.95.

A historical account covering pronunciation, spelling, usage, American and English, and including words, phrases, proper names, slang, etc. Readable. Bibliographical footnotes. This is a distillation of the author's three-volume set, with some updating to show recent changes in the language.

400 Pei, Mario Andrew. The story of language. Rev. ed. Lippincott, 1965. 491p. $7.50; paper (New Amer. Lib.) $.95.

For reading or reference. Discusses the history and elements of language and relationships of languages. Contains a section on an international language, a word list, and an index.

Dictionaries

General English-Language Dictionaries

401 Americanisms, a dictionary of selected Americanisms on historical principles, by Mitford M. Mathews. Univ. of Chicago Pr., 1966. 304p. $5.95; paper $1.95.

An abridgment of *A Dictionary of Americanisms on Historical Principles,* 1951. Includes words originating elsewhere but deriving new meanings in America. Bibliography.

402 Funk and Wagnalls Standard dictionary of the English language. International ed. Funk, 1966. 2v. $35; 1v. ed. $24.50.

Not exhaustive, but useful with Webster's Third because of its discriminative comment. Aims to keep up with new vocabulary, especially with scientific and technical terms, and includes proper names and foreign phrases all in one alphabet.

403 Murray, *Sir* James Augustus Henry, ed. Shorter Oxford English dictionary on historical principles. Prepared by William Little, H. W. Fowler, J. Coulson. Rev. and edited by C. T. Onions. 3d ed. with addenda. Oxford Univ. Pr., 1955. 2515p. $32; 2v. ed. $33.75.

Although this is the abridged edition of the *Oxford English Dictionary,* it serves also as a supplement to it because of the addition of new words.

404 Random House dictionary of the English language. Jess Stein, editor in chief. Laurence Urdang, managing ed. Random House, 1966. 2059p. $25.

An attempt to catch up with our expanding vocabulary. Not exhaustive. Definitions are more informal than those in Webster's Unabridged. Lists important plays, books, and persons, and adds useful tables of volcanoes, ocean depths, rivers by length, etc. Includes an atlas and concise dictionaries of Spanish, French, German, and Italian.

405 Webster's Third new international dictionary of the English language, unabridged. A Merriam-Webster. Editor in chief, Philip Babcock Gove and the Merriam-Webster editorial staff. Merriam, 1961. 2662p. $47.50; 2v. ed. $52.50.

Often criticized for its lack of preferred usage and for its acceptance of words not usually regarded as proper English. Libraries will wish to retain the second edition as well.

Abbreviations and Acronyms

406 De Sola, Ralph. Abbreviations dictionary: abbreviations, acronyms, contractions, signs & symbols defined, including civil and military time signals, Greek alphabet, international civil aircraft markings, numbered abbreviations, proof-reader's marks, punctuation and diacritical marks, radio alphabet, Roman nu-

merals, and ship's bell time signals, etc. New rev. and enl. international ed. (Duell) Meredith, 1967. 298p. $6.95.

A useful but less comprehensive work than that published by Gale Research Company.

407 Gale Research Company. Acronyms and initialisms dictionary; a guide to alphabetic designations, contractions, acronyms, initialisms, and similar condensed appellations; covering: aerospace, associations, biochemistry, business and trade, domestic and international affairs, education, electronics, genetics, government, labor, medicine, military, pharmacy, physiology, politics, religion, science, societies, sports, technical drawings and specifications, transportation, and other fields. 2d ed. edited by Robert C. Thomas, James M. Ethridge, and Frederick G. Ruffner, Jr. Contributing eds., Edwin B. Steen and others. Gale Res., 1965. 767p. $15.

Includes the most often encountered foreign terms, but is largely a compilation relating to the United States.

408 Schwartz, Robert J. Complete dictionary of abbreviations. Crowell, 1955. 211p. $6.95.

Includes Signs and Symbols, Braille Alphabet and Numerals, Roman Numerals, Letter Symbols for Chemical Engineering. Greek Alphabet, etc., in appendixes.

Etymology

409 Holt, Alfred Hubbard. Phrase and word origins; a study of familiar expressions. Rev. ed. Dover, 1961. 254p. Paper $1.50.

Comments on the history and use of picturesque words and phrases.

410 Onions, Charles Talbut, and others, eds. Oxford dictionary of English etymology. Oxford Univ. Pr., 1966. 1024p. $16.50.

A modern and comprehensive etymological dictionary of the English language. Based on the *Oxford English Dictionary* and brought up to date. Includes some words of American origin, as well as personal and geographical names, and gives pronunciation.

411 Skeat, Walter William. A concise etymological dictionary of the English language. New and corr. impression. Oxford Univ. Pr., 1911. 663p. $4; paper $2.95 (Putnam, 1963).

Shorter than the author's *Etymological Dictionary* (below) and entirely rewritten. Gives derivations of words, but omits histories of their use. Appendix contains same information as in the larger and older work.

412 ———An etymological dictionary of the English language. New rev. and enl. ed. Oxford Univ. Pr., 1910. 780p. $11.20.

Frequently reprinted. A standard work, scholarly and historical. For smaller libraries, the author's *Concise Etymological Dictionary* (above) may suffice. Appendix contains lists of prefixes, suffixes, homonyms, doublets, selected lists of Latin and Greek words, and the distribution of words according to the languages from which they are derived.

Proverbs

413 Smith, William George. Oxford dictionary of English proverbs, with an introduction by Janet E. Heseltine. 2d ed. rev. throughout by *Sir* Paul Harvey. Oxford Univ. Pr., 1948. 740p. $7.70.

Provides an excellent supplement to the various books of quotations. Proverbs are arranged by the most significant word, with many cross references.

414 Stevenson, Burton Egbert. Macmillan book of proverbs. Macmillan, 1965 (1948). 2957p. $25.

A subject arrangement of proverbs, maxims, and familiar phrases; a companion volume to Stevenson's *Home Book of Quotations*. Has a very full index.

Rhyming Dictionaries

415 Johnson, Burges. New rhyming dictionary and poets' handbook. Rev. ed. Harper, 1957. 464p. $5.95; lib. bdg. $5.11.

Easy to use. Arranged by one-, two-, and three-syllable

words, and includes definitions and illustrations of the various poetic forms and meters.

416 Reed, Langford. Writer's rhyming dictionary. Writer, 1961. 244p. $2.95.

Small but useful. Arranged by rhyme sounds of one-syllable rhymes, or words in which the final and accented syllable is a rhyme, and by two-syllable rhymes.

Slang

417 Berrey, Lester V., and Van den Bark, Melvin. American thesaurus of slang; a complete reference book of colloquial speech. 2d ed. Crowell, 1953. 1272p. $15.

Comprehensive list, divided into sections for general slang and colloquialisms, the language of particular groups, and slang origins. Well indexed.

418 Partridge, Eric. Dictionary of slang and unconventional English; colloquialisms and catch-phrases, solecisms and catachreses, nicknames, vulgarisms and such Americanisms as have been naturalized. 6th ed. rev. and enl. Macmillan, 1967. 2v. $17.50.

The standard work on the subject; historical approach.

419 ———A dictionary of the underworld, British & American; being the vocabularies of crooks, criminals, racketeers, beggars and tramps, convicts, the commercial underworld, the drug traffic, the white slave traffic, spivs. Macmillan, 1961. 817p. $15.

Slang from America and the United Kingdom. "A dictionary planned on historical lines."

420 Wentworth, Harold, and Flexner, Stuart Berg, comps. and eds. Dictionary of American slang, with a supplement by Stuart Berg Flexner. Supplemented ed. Crowell, 1967. 718p. $7.95.

Quotations and definitions cover all shades of the meanings

of words used by college students, beatniks, hoboes, and other social groups. Basic reference tool for American slang. New material contained in a 48-page supplement. Appendix contains word lists for affixes, reduplications, Pig Latin, onomatopoeia, nicknames, group names, and a selected bibliography.

Synonyms

421 Roget, Peter Mark. Roget's International thesaurus. 3d ed. Crowell, 1962. 1258p. $5.95.

The standard thesaurus or word book, arranged by ideas. This edition has the "pinpoint" index for locating the precise word quickly.

422 Webster's Dictionary of synonyms. A Merriam-Webster. A dictionary of discriminated synonyms, with antonyms and analogous and contrasted words. Merriam, 1951. 907p. $6.75.

Perhaps the most useful of the dictionaries of synonyms. Includes a Survey of the History of English Synonymy.

Usage

423 Copperud, Roy H. A dictionary of usage and style; the reference guide for professional writers, reporters, editors, teachers and students. 1st ed. Hawthorn, 1964. 452p. $6.95.

A helpful guide in avoiding errors of usage. Troublesome words and expressions are arranged in one alphabet along with major articles on collectives, punctuation marks, gerund construction, modifiers, possessive forms, etc.

424 Evans, Bergen, and Evans, Cornelia. A dictionary of contemporary American usage. Random House, 1957. 567p. $6.95.

A highly personal work displaying scholarship and wit. Includes British usage. The authors "are prejudiced in favor of literary forms," but list nonliterary forms when there is evidence that they have been accepted. Arrangement of words, phrases, clichés, grammar, punctuation, etc., is in one alphabet.

425 Follett, Wilson. Modern American usage; a guide. Edited and completed by Jacques Barzun and others. 1st ed. Hill & Wang, 1966. 436p. $7.50.

A helpful addition to books on good usage. Not so easy to use as Evans, and less compliant in the acceptance of new forms. Appendixes discuss confusion and conflict in use of "shall and will" and punctuation.

426 Fowler, Henry Watson. A dictionary of modern English usage, 2d ed. rev. by *Sir* Ernest Gowers. Oxford Univ. Pr., 1965. 725p. $5.

There are some alterations, omissions, and additions, primarily for the purpose of bringing the work into focus with present-day usage. A new edition of a standard work.

427 U.S. Government Printing Office. Style manual. Govt. Print. Off., 1959. 496p. $2.75.

This is primarily a Government Printing Office printers' stylebook. The rules are based on principles of good usage and custom in the printing trades, but the work is valuable in answering all general questions. Includes a guide to the typography of foreign languages.

Foreign-Language Dictionaries

► A small collection of bilingual dictionaries in the classical and major modern European languages is desirable. In a locality where there are other language groups, libraries should also provide bilingual dictionaries for these languages. The addition of a standard foreign-language dictionary will often prove useful for some encyclopedic information not readily available in English works.

Chinese

428 Mathews, Robert Henry. Chinese-English dictionary. Rev. American ed. Harvard Univ. Pr., 1943. 1226p. $10.

429 ———A Chinese-English dictionary. Rev. English index. Harvard Univ. Pr., 1944. 186p. $4.50.

First title compiled for the China Inland Mission; second title published for Harvard's Yenching Institute. The second serves as a guide to the use of the first.

French

430 Larousse modern French-English dictionary, by Marguerite-Marie Dubois and others. Tudor, 1960. 2v. in 1, 768p., 751p. $7.95.

A good standard equivalency dictionary.

431 New Cassell's French dictionary, French-English; English-French. Compiled by Denis Girard. Compl. rev. Funk, 1962. 2v. in 1, 762p., 655p. $7.50.

Phonetic pronunciation. Includes proper names, tables of English and French irregular verbs, and English and French definitions.

432 Petit Larousse, dictionnaire encyclopédique pour tous. Schoenhof, 1967. 1795p. $8.95.

Illustrations in black and white and color. Portraits and maps are included. Separate lists of personal and place-names. Earlier edition titled *Nouveau petit Larousse illustré.*

German

433 Betteridge, Harold T., ed. New Cassell's German dictionary; German-English, English-German. Rev. ed. Funk, 1962. 2v. in 1, 629p., 619p. $7.50.

Useful appendixes of abbreviations, proper names, and irregular verbs.

434 Brockhaus illustrated German-English, English-German dictionary. McGraw-Hill, 1959–60. 2v. in 1. $7.95.

Good standard dictionary with some illustrations.

435 New Wildhagen German dictionary, German-English, English-German. Follett, 1965. 2v. in 1, 1296p., 1061p. $19.95.

The English-German section uses phonetic pronunciation and has a list of geographical and proper names, and a section on German grammar. Scientific and technical terms are included. The appendix in the German-English section includes a pronouncing vocabulary of proper names.

436 Der Sprach-Brockhaus. 7th rev. and enl. ed. S. F. Book Imports, 1961. 799p. $6.

Illustrated all-German dictionary.

Greek

437 Swanson, Donald C., and Djaferis, S. P. Vocabulary of modern spoken Greek; English-Greek, Greek-English. Univ. of Minnesota Pr., 1959. 408p. $5.

Includes useful sections on names of food and drink, weights and measures, and greetings for students or tourists.

Hebrew

438 Alcalay, Reuben. Complete English-Hebrew dictionary. Prayer Bk. Pr., 1963. 2v. $14.95 each.

Considered the best dictionary of an evolving language. Gives idiomatic usage in both English and Hebrew. Includes some proper names.

Italian

439 Hazon, Mario, ed. Garzanti comprehensive Italian-English; English-Italian dictionary. McGraw-Hill, 1963 (c1961). 2099p. $12.50.

The vocabulary of more than 100,000 entries includes pronunciation, idioms, and variations in usage. Abbreviations in common use in Italy and in English-speaking countries and proper names common in form in both languages are given in interesting appendixes.

440 Reynolds, Barbara, ed. Cambridge Italian dictionary. Cambridge Univ. Pr., 1962. v.1, Italian-English, 897p., $32.50; v.2, English-Italian (in prep.).

Planned as a revision to Alfred Hoare's *An Italian Dictionary*. The vocabulary represents literary and spoken Italian. Obsolescence and special meanings are indicated.

Japanese

441 Kenkyusha's New Japanese-English dictionary. Edited by Senkichiro Katsumata. New ed. Kenkyusha, 1954. 2136p. $15.

Japanese words are arranged alphabetically in transliterated form, followed by Japanese characters and their English equivalents. Includes supplemental tables.

442 Nelson, Andrew Nathaniel. Modern reader's Japanese-English character dictionary. Tuttle, 1962. 1048p. $14.50.

Japanese characters precede the transliterations, which are arranged alphabetically. Extensive appendixes. More helpful than the Kenkyusha dictionary (above) for the non-Japanese interested in understanding the language in addition to merely identifying words.

Latin

443 Cassell's New Latin dictionary; Latin-English, English-Latin. Rev. ed. Funk, 1959. 883p. $7.50.

Contains proper names in the general vocabulary with dates and identifying phrases. Sometimes brief biographies are included.

444 A Latin dictionary founded on Andrews' Edition of Freund's Latin dictionary (1879). Rev. by Charlton T. Lewis and Charles Short. Oxford Univ. Pr., 1962. 2019p. $12.80.

Includes quotations from classical authors.

Polish

445 Bulas, K., Thomas, L.L., and Whitfield, F. J. Kosciusko

Foundation dictionary: English-Polish, Polish-English. The Foundation, 1960–62. 2v. $10 each.

Phonetic pronunciation is used for English entries.

Portuguese

446 Aliandro, Hygino. Compact dictionary of the Portuguese and English languages. McKay, 1963. 2v. $5 the set; $2.75 each.

Each volume has a concise discussion of grammar, Portuguese in one, English in the other. The special features differ in each volume. For example, a classical dictionary, national flowers, and forms of address appear in the Portuguese-English volume; proper names, abbreviations, and tables of weights and measures appear in the English-Portuguese volume.

447 New Appleton dictionary of the English and Portuguese languages. Edited by Antônio Houaiss and Catherine B. Avery. Appleton, 1964. 2v. in 1, 636p., 665p. $14.95.

Phonetic pronunciation is used. There are tables of abbreviations commonly used in Portuguese, foreign words used without change in Portuguese, numerals, and irregular verbs.

Russian

448 The learner's English-Russian dictionary, by S. Folomkiva and H. Weiser. Mass. Inst. of Technology, 1963. 744p. $7.95; paper $2.95.

449 The learner's Russian-English dictionary, by B. A. Lapidus and S. V. Shevtosova, with foreword and article on orthography by Morris Halle. Mass. Inst. of Technology, 1963. 688p. $7.95; paper $2.95.

Both volumes are planned for the needs of beginning students in each language.

450 Müller, Vladimir Karlovich, comp. English-Russian dictionary. 7th ed. rev. and enl. Dutton, 1965. 1192p. $9.95.

Useful for scientific and technical terms as well as general terms. See also Smirnitsky's *Russian-English Dictionary* (below).

451 Smirnitsky, Alexander Ivanovich, comp. Russian-English dictionary. 7th ed. rev. Dutton, 1966. 766p. $8.95.
Useful companion volume to Müller's *English-Russian Dictionary* (above).

452 A phrase and sentence dictionary of spoken Russian; Russian-English, English-Russian. Dover, 1958. 573p. Paper $3.
First published as a U.S. War Department Technical Manual, TM30-944. Includes special vocabularies, such as geographical names, national holidays, foods, and abbreviations.

Spanish

453 Cassell's Spanish-English, English-Spanish dictionary. Funk, 1960. 1477p. $7.50.
Appendixes of irregular Spanish and English verbs, common Spanish and English abbreviations, etc.

454 Crowell's Spanish-English and English-Spanish dictionary, by Gerd A. Gillhoff. Crowell, 1963. 1261p. $4.95.
Includes Latin Americanisms and many special vocabularies. Also has outlines of the grammar of both languages and an illustrated vocabulary builder.

455 Real Academia Española, Madrid. Diccionario de la lengua española. 18th ed. Editorial Espasa Calpe or S. F. Book Imports, 1956. 1370p. $5.75.
An authority for current Spanish. In this edition recent words in science and technology have been added to the vocabulary.

456 Velázquez de la Cadena, Mariano, and others. Velázquez Spanish and English dictionary. New rev. ed. Follett, 1964. 1480p. $7.95.
A synopsis of Spanish grammar precedes the entries in this dictionary of equivalencies.

14
Literature

Bibliographies and Indexes

457 Bateson, Frederick W. A guide to English literature. Aldine, 1965. 259p. $5; paper $1.25 (Doubleday, 1965).

Essays on each literary period, with annotated bibliographies to 1960.

458 Cambridge bibliography of English literature. Edited by F. W. Bateson. Cambridge Univ. Pr., 1941–1957. 5v. $55. v.1–3,5 $13.50 each; v.4 $5.50.

Indispensable bibliography for libraries doing much work in English literature.

459 Cook, Dorothy Elizabeth, and Monro, Isabel S. Short story index; an index to 60,000 stories in 4,320 collections. Wilson, 1953. 1553p. $16.

———— ————Supplement, 1950–1954. Compiled by Dorothy E. Cook and Estelle A. Fidell. Wilson, 1956. 394p. $8. (Indexes 9575 stories in 549 collections.)

———— ————Supplement, 1955–1958. Compiled by Estelle A. Fidell and Esther V. Flory. Wilson, 1960. 341p. $8. (Indexes 6392 stories in 376 collections.)

———— ————Supplement, 1959–1963. Compiled by Estelle A. Fidell. Wilson, 1965. 487p. $12. (Indexes 9068 stories in 582 collections.)

These indexes provide an invaluable clue to short stories in collections. Indexing is by author, title, and subject of the short story. A list of collections indexed provides a useful buying guide for the library.

460 Essay and general literature index, 1900–1933. Wilson, 1934. 1952p. $48. Subsequent volumes are: 1934–40, 1362p. $48; 1941–47, 1908p. $48; 1948–54, 2306p. $48; 1955–59,

1421p. $48; 1960–64, 1589p. $48. Annual subscription $16.

This index is published semiannually with bound annual and five-year cumulations. It indexes, by author and subject, essays appearing in collections from 1900 on. Thus it forms a useful adjunct to the card catalog of any library.

461 Granger, Edith. Granger's Index to poetry. Edited by William F. Bernhardt. 5th ed. compl. rev. and enl. Columbia Univ. Pr., 1962. 2123p. $65.

———— ————Supplement to the 5th ed., indexing anthologies from July 1, 1960 to December 31, 1965. Edited by William F. Bernhardt and Kathryn W. Sewny. Columbia Univ. Pr., 1967. 416p. $35.

Symbols for anthologies indexed are given in combined title and first-line index. There are separate indexes by author and by subject.

462 Sutton, Roberta (Briggs). Speech index. 4th ed. Scarecrow, 1966. 947p. $20.

The 4th edition incorporates all the materials in the three previous editions: 1935, 1935–55, and 1956–62, with additional titles in this field published from 1900 through 1965. Indexes speeches by orator, type of speech, and by subject, with a selected list of titles given in the appendix. Particularly useful for the amateur speaker in locating suggestions on how to prepare a speech and models he can adapt to his needs.

Encyclopedias

463 Benét, William Rose, ed. Reader's encyclopedia. 2d ed. Crowell, 1965. 1118p. $8.95.

A completely revised edition of a basic reference book useful in libraries of every size and type. Covers world literature. Entries on authors, titles, characters, allusions, literary movements, etc.

464 Cambridge history of English literature. Edited by A. W.

Ward and A. R. Waller. Cambridge Univ. Pr., 1907–33. 15v. $95; $7 each.

An important general history. May be supplemented by the *Oxford History of English Literature* (below). Original edition included excellent bibliographies and, if owned, should be retained. Bibliographies now published separately (see no. 458).

465 Oxford history of English literature. Edited by Frank Percy Wilson and Bonamy Dobrée. Oxford Univ. Pr., 1945–   . 12v. (Incomplete)

v.2: pt.I, Bennett, H. S. Chaucer and the fifteenth century. 1947. 326p. $8.25; pt.II, Chambers, E. K. English literature at the close of the middle ages. 1947. 247p. $7.

v.3, Lewis, C. S. English literature in the sixteenth century, excluding drama. 1954. 696p. $10.

v.5, Bush, Douglas. English literature in the earlier seventeenth century, 1600–1660. 1946. 621p. $10.50.

v.7, Dobrée, Bonamy. English literature in the early eighteenth century, 1700–1740. 1959. 701p. $11.

v.9, Renwick, W. L. English literature, 1789–1815. 1963. 293p. $7.

v.10, Jack, Ian. English literature, 1815–1832. 1963. 643p. $11.50.

v.12, Stewart, J. I. M. Eight modern writers. 1963. 704p. $11.

Updates the *Cambridge History of English Literature* (above) and, when finished, may supersede it. Excellent bibliographies included.

466 Herzberg, Max J., and the staff of the Thomas Y. Crowell Company. Reader's encyclopedia of American literature. Crowell, 1962. 1280p. $12.95.

Essential facts about American and Canadian writers and writing from colonial times to 1962 are provided in this comprehensive one-volume reference book. Includes articles on authors, novels, plays, poems, stories, literary groups, newspapers, and places and terms associated with literature.

467 Literary history of the United States. Eds., Robert E. Spiller

and others. 3d ed. rev. Macmillan, 1963. 2v. in 1, 1511p. $15.
————Bibliography supplement. Edited by R. M. Ludwig. 1964. 268p. $15.

The standard work on the subject, giving a comprehensive survey from colonial times to date and including a selected bibliography. Supplemental volume provides bibliographic essays on various aspects of the field, including individual authors.

468 Sampson, George. Concise Cambridge history of English literature. 2d ed. Cambridge Univ. Pr., 1962. 1071p. $6.50.

A survey history based on the 14-volume *Cambridge History of English Literature*, with a new chapter on "The Age of T. S. Eliot."

469 Steinberg, Sigfrid H., ed. Cassell's Encyclopaedia of world literature. Funk, 1953. 2v. $25; $12.50 each.

Scholarly, signed articles about literary terms, schools of writing, national literatures, and specific works. Author biographies are excellent for identification of lesser-known authors and works. Articles have multilingual bibliographies.

470 Temple, Ruth Z., and Tucker, M. A library of literary criticism; modern British literature. Ungar, 1966. 3v. $35.

Designed to supplement C. W. Moulton's *Library of Literary Criticism of English and American Authors* (Peter Smith, 1967. 8v. $10 each), giving excerpts of criticism from book reviews, journals, and biographies.

Dictionaries and Handbooks

471 Beckson, Karl, and Ganz, Arthur. A reader's guide to literary terms; a dictionary. Farrar, 1960. 230p. $4.95; paper $1.95 (Noonday).

Definitions and little essays on generic literary terms, the emphasis being on English literature. This is one of several currently available so-called dictionaries of literary terms, all competently put together but none worth labeling as "best." They all supplement one another in various ways. Many terms have to be looked for elsewhere, even if one has all the dictionaries. Two later ones are:

472 Scott, Arthur Finley. Current literary terms; a concise dictionary of their origin and use. St. Martin's, 1966. 324p. $4.95.

473 Yelland, Hedley Lowry, and others, comps. A handbook of literary terms. Citadel, 1966. 221p. Paper $1.95.

474 Brewer, Ebenezer C. Dictionary of phrase and fable. 8th ed. rev. by John Freeman. Harper, 1964. 970p. $7.50.
One can use this for years and still be amazed at the amount of information it includes on linguistic, literary, historical, biographical, and other subjects. The entry can be a phrase, name, title, quotation, proverb, or generic category (e.g., "Dying sayings"). In a class by itself, even if many of its entries can be found elsewhere with searching.

475 Burke, William J., and Howe, Will D. American authors and books, 1640 to the present day. Augmented and rev. by Irving R. Weiss. Crown, 1962. 834p. $8.50.
Concise and useful information about authors and their works, from the best to the least known. Includes related items such as literary societies, magazines, etc.

476 Freeman, William. Dictionary of fictional characters. Writer, 1963. 458p. $6.95.
Identifies about 20,000 characters created by some 500 authors over a six-century period.

477 Harvey, *Sir* Paul. Oxford companion to English literature. 4th ed. Oxford Univ. Pr., 1967. 961p. $12.50.
English authors, literary works, and literary societies are stressed, but non-English persons and literary items are included when allied to English literature. The result is a handbook of

widely miscellaneous, English-literature-oriented information.

478 Hornstein, Lillian, and others, eds. Reader's companion to
world literature. Holt, 1956. 493p. $6.95.
   Dictionary arrangement of short entries on authors, literary
types, terms, and periods, covering all literatures and based on
the editors' judgment of what is needed for literary knowledge.
The approach is that of the Great Books and college syllabi.

479 Magill, Frank N., ed. Cyclopedia of literary characters.
Harper, 1964. 1280p. $9.95; lib. bdg. $8.97 net.
   Identifies and describes more than 16,000 characters, grouped
under the title of the literary work in which they appear. An
author index and a complete-name index facilitate ready-reference use. Also published under title: *Masterplots Cyclopedia of
Literary Characters*.

480 New century handbook of English literature. Rev. ed. Edited
by Clarence L. Barnhart. Appleton, 1956. 1167p. $14.95.
   Based largely on the *New Century Cyclopedia of Names*.
There are entries for biography, allusions, titles, and characters.
Somewhat more inclusive than the *Oxford Companion to Eng-
lish Literature*.

481 Opie, Iona (Archibald), and Opie, Peter, eds. Oxford dictionary of nursery rhymes. Oxford Univ. Pr., 1951. 467p.
$10.50.
   A scholarly collection of nursery rhymes with notes and explanations concerning history, literary associations, social uses,
and possible portrayal of real people.

482 Smith, Horatio. Columbia dictionary of modern European
literature. Columbia Univ. Pr., 1947. 899p. est. $15.
   Discusses 31 national literatures and the chief works of their
representative authors from about 1870 to modern times.
Signed articles are accompanied, in most instances, by bibliographies.

Quotation Books

483 Bartlett, John. Familiar quotations. 14th ed. Little, 1968.
1614p. $10.
A standard collection with quotations arranged chronologically by authors. Excellent index.

484 Simpson, James B. Contemporary quotations. Crowell, 1964.
500p. $6.95.
Supplements the standard collections of quotations. Contains
more than 2400 quotable remarks made between the years
1950 and 1964. Categories include politics and government,
business, law, science, the arts, travel, and family life. Separate
indexes for source and subject.

485 Stevenson, Burton Egbert. Home book of quotations, classical
and modern, selected and arranged. 10th ed. Dodd, 1967.
2816p. $35.
One of the most comprehensive and useful of the many books
of quotations. Arrangement is by subject, with a very detailed
index. A first purchase for any reference collection.

Poetry

486 Perrine, Laurence. Sound and sense: an introduction to
poetry. 2d ed. Harcourt, 1963. 334p. Paper $3.75.
For those readers who wish to learn how to appreciate and
evaluate poetry. Brief essays are followed by liberal examples.

487 Preminger, Alexander, ed. Encyclopedia of poetry and po-
etics. Princeton Univ. Pr., 1965. 906p. $25.
Extensive articles, signed by modern authorities in the field
of literary criticism, about all phases of poetry, i.e., history,
types, movements, prosody, critical terminology, and literary
schools. Bibliographies are appended to almost every entry.

488 Spender, Stephen, and Hall, Donald, eds. Concise encyclo-

pedia of English and American poets and poetry. Hawthorn, 1963. 415p. $15.

Includes articles on techniques and form but is basically biographical. Many full-page portraits. Bibliography.

Shakespeare

489 Bartlett, John. A complete concordance or verbal index to words, phrases and passages in the dramatic works of Shakespeare with a supplementary concordance to the poems. St. Martin's, 1965 (c1894). 1910p. $30.

An unrivaled work.

490 Campbell, Oscar James, and Quinn, Edward G., eds. Reader's encyclopedia of Shakespeare. Crowell, 1966. 1014p. $15.

A compendium of criticism and information on all aspects of Shakespeare's works. Sources are given at the end of many articles. Appendixes include a chronology of events related to the life and works of Shakespeare, transcripts of documents, genealogical table of Houses of York and Lancaster, and a 30-page selected bibliography.

491 Halliday, Frank Ernest. A Shakespeare companion, 1564–1964. Rev. ed. Schocken, 1964. 569p. $10; 565p. paper $2.25 (Penguin).

Includes information on persons, plays, characters, and theater contemporary to Shakespeare, as well as on matters pertaining to Shakespeare himself. Also contains genealogical tables of the Shakespeare family, and pertaining to Shakespeare's English historical plays. Bibliography and illustrations are in the back.

492 Kökeritz, Helge. Shakespeare's names: a pronouncing dictionary. Yale Univ. Pr., 1959. 100p. $2.50.

Phonetic transcriptions only of the proper names appearing in Shakespeare's works.

493 Onions, Charles T. A Shakespeare glossary. 2d rev. ed. Oxford Univ. Pr., 1963. 264p. $4.

Gives definitions and illustrations of words or senses of words now obsolete, explanations involving unfamiliar allusions, and proper names. A six-page addendum has been made to the 1919 edition.

494 Stevenson, Burton Egbert. Home book of Shakespeare quotations. Scribner, 1965 (c1937). 2055p. $18.95.

A subject guide with exact citations to the Globe edition of Shakespeare's plays and poems. A concordance is also provided.

National Literatures

General

495 Priestley, J. B. Literature and Western man. Harper, 1960. 512p. $10; paper $2.75.

An evaluation of all forms of Western (including Russian) literature from the invention of printing to the mid-twentieth century. Contains, in an appendix, brief paragraphs of biographical data on authors no longer living. Indexed.

Australian

496 Hadgraft, Cecil. Australian literature, a critical account to 1955. Dufour, 1961. 302p. $5.50.

A survey history from early colonial days to 1955.

French

497 Cazamian, Louis François. History of French literature. Oxford Univ. Pr., 1955. 464p. $8.25; paper $2.95.

Critical interpretation of literature from the medieval ninth century to 1950, arranged chronologically. Types of literature are discussed, as well as individual authors and their works. Indexed.

498 Harvey, *Sir* Paul, and Heseltine, Janet E., eds. Oxford com-

panion to French literature. Oxford Univ. Pr., 1959. 771p. $13.

6000 entries of varying length encompass the range of French literature up to World War II, including the work of some historians, philosophers, and scientists. Works are listed with dates of first publication. Cross references. Appended bibliography.

German

499 Rose, Ernst. History of German literature. New York Univ. Pr., 1960. 353p. $6.50; paper $2.75.

A literary history developed to show the effect of history on literature and vice versa. Selective bibliography of works of and about the literature in translation. Index.

Italian

500 Wilkins, Ernest Hatch. History of Italian literature. Harvard Univ. Pr., 1954. 523p. $9.

A brief survey, from the thirteenth century to the mid-twentieth, of Italian literature "of particular interest to the English-speaking world." Some biographical information together with critical interpretation of the work. Listing of authors *not* treated and of literary periods; bibliography of books in English about Italian literature. Indexed.

Russian

501 Mirsky, Dmitrii S. A history of Russian literature. Knopf, 1949. 518p. $6.95; paper $1.65 (Vintage).

Eleventh-century to early twentieth-century poetry, drama, and fiction. Biographical details and critical commentary are given. Extensively indexed.

502 Slonim, Mark. Soviet Russian literature: writers and problems. Oxford Univ. Pr., 1964. 365p. $7.50. Rev. ed. Paper $2.25.

Major, widely known authors are discussed in chapters devoted entirely to them, while trends and cultural influences, together with critical comment on minor writers, are dealt with separately. Works are not indexed by title, but included under author's name. Notes include a selected bibliography of available English translations and criticism.

Spanish

503 Chandler, Richard E., and Schwartz, Kessel. New history of Spanish literature. Louisiana State Univ. Pr., 1961. 696p. $10.
Cultural background, geography, and language formation are discussed as a setting for a complete history of types of Spanish literature—poetry, drama, fiction, and nonfiction prose. Appendixes include a general historical chronology. Bibliography and extensive index.

Spanish-American

504 Anderson-Imbert, Enrique. Spanish American literature. Wayne State Univ. Pr., 1963. 616p. $17.50.
Six centuries of literature written in Spanish in the Americas are considered in chronological order. Historical and cultural framework discussed. Author index only. Selected bibliography.

Classical Literature

General

505 Feder, Lillian. Crowell's Handbook of classical literature. Crowell, 1964. 448p. $6.95.
Dictionary arrangement of terms, persons, gods, and places relative to the study of Greek and Roman literature. Famous books are analyzed book by book, and plays, scene by scene. Gives historical background. Extensive cross references.

506 Harvey, *Sir* Paul. Oxford companion to classical literature. Oxford Univ. Pr., 1937. 2d ed. 468p. $5.75.
Useful for identifying geographical, historical, mythological,

and political backgrounds that are relevant to the study and understanding of the literature of Greece and Rome. Extensively cross referenced. Appendixes include maps, table of weights and measures, and a date chart.

507 Oxford classical dictionary. Edited by M. Cary and others. Oxford Univ. Pr. (c1949). 971p. $14.50.

A standard information source for art and archaeology, history, literature, mythology, philosophy, science, etc. of the classical world. Articles are signed and include bibliographies.

508 Peck, Harry T., ed. Harper's Dictionary of classical literature and antiquities. Cooper Sq., 1923. 1701p. Lib. bdg. $19.95.

A dictionary arrangement of predominantly short articles which identify authors, works, literary allusions and terminology, mythology, and other items useful for reference in classical fields. Bibliography and good illustrations for many articles. Although the book is old, it is still valuable.

Greek

509 Hadas, Moses. History of Greek literature. Columbia Univ. Pr., 1950. 327p. $7.50; paper $1.95.

Coverage extends up to the age of Justinian, and includes drama, oratory, history, philosophy, and religious writing. Bibliographic notes. Index.

510 Rose, Herbert J. A handbook of Greek literature. Rev. ed. Dutton, 1964. 458p. $7.95; paper $1.85.

A historical and critical discussion of the major authors; less well-known writers are considered in footnotes. Index does not include titles of individual works mentioned, only the authors—a fact that makes the book somewhat limited for use as a reference tool.

Latin

511 Duff, John W. Literary history of Rome. Barnes & Noble.

v.1, From the origins to the close of the Golden Age. 3d ed. 1964. $8.75; paper $2.95; v.2, Silver Age: from Tiberius to Hadrian. 2d ed. 1960. $10; paper (1964) $3.95.

First published in 1909 (v.1) and 1927 (v.2), this still ranks with the very best general histories of ancient Latin literature.

512 Hadas, Moses. History of Latin literature. Columbia Univ. Pr., 1952. 474p. $7.50; paper (1964) $2.45.

Discussion by a leading classical scholar of Latin literature from its beginning to the sixth century A.D., covering both the well-known and the lesser writers. Many extracts. Bibliographic notes. Extensive index.

15
Geography, Travel, and Archaeology

General Works

513 Columbia Lippincott gazetteer of the world. Edited by Leon E. Seltzer with the geographical staff of Columbia University Press and with the cooperation of the American Geographical Society, with 1961 supplement. Columbia Univ. Pr., 1962. 2148p. $75.

A standard reference tool. Includes alphabetical listings of place-names, mountains, rivers, and oceans; gives population, height above sea level, approximate location, trade, industry, communications, and other pertinent facts. Population figures for the United States have been updated to 1960.

514 Concise encyclopedia of archaeology. Edited by Leonard Cottrell. Hawthorn, 1960. 512p. $15.

This authoritative reference tool, an epitome of the subject, covers extant discoveries and technical methods employed by all recognized archaeologists up to the time of publication. Bibliographies. Illustrations, many in color.

515 Freeman, Otis Willard, and Morris, John, eds. World geography. 2d ed. McGraw-Hill, 1965. 710p. $9.95.
    A general geography on the undergraduate college or general adult level. Unfortunately, illustrations are not always placed near the text they illustrate.

516 Webster's Geographical dictionary. Rev. ed. Merriam, 1964. 1293p. $8.50.
    A good one-volume gazetteer, revised frequently. Gives pronunciation.

Atlases

► The number of general world atlases needed by a library will, of course, depend upon its size and the nature of its clientele. A small library may acquire only one or two, but it should make a special effort to see that at least one is quite up to date. The atlases listed here are considered very good. Smaller and less expensive atlases are also available. For an idea of what will be found in atlases other than those listed below, see Walsh, *General World Atlases in Print: A Comparative Analysis* (below).

517 Encyclopaedia Britannica world atlas. Encyclopaedia Britannica, 1966. 418p. $29.50.
    Accurate, attractive, and easy-to-read maps suitable for students of junior and senior high school level and for adults. Contains political-physical maps for the world and special regions: Eurasia, Africa, Australia and Oceania, South America, and North America. About 40 percent of the coverage is on the United States. "World Scene" section includes maps showing world distribution by population, birth rate, death rate, languages, literacy, etc. "Geographical Summaries" gives statistics by regions and political units; the world's largest lakes, longest rivers, etc. are noted under "Geographical Comparisons." The

atlas also contains a glossary of geographical terms and a gazetteer index. Continuous revision. Published annually.

518 Medallion world atlas. Hammond, 1966. 415p. $19.95.
     One of the most comprehensive of the Hammond atlases.
Contains an alphabetical list of countries, states, colonial pos-
sessions, and other major geographical areas, noting for each
its area, capital or chief town, and population, with the source
and date of the latter. Includes a 31-page pictorial account of
the universe, depicting man's relation to the universe, to the
earth, and to his environment. The arrangement of the material
in the bulk of the volume is by continent, then country, state,
or province. All geographically related information pertaining
to a country or region appears on pages adjacent to the ones
containing a large multicolored political map (with its own
gazetteer index) and a series of smaller typographical, economic,
transportation, and other special maps. Statistical data for each
include area, population, monetary unit, major language, and
an illustration of its national flag in color. For the 50 states in
the United States information featured includes highest point,
date settled, date of admission to the Union, popular name,
name of state flower and state bird, and a highway map. A comprehensive overall A–Z world index of all localities on the maps
is provided, as is a glossary of geographical terms, information
on map projection, and world statistical tables of oceans and
seas, the principal lakes, islands, mountains, great ship canals,
and the longest rivers.

519 National Geographic atlas of the world. Melville B. Gros-
     venor, editor in chief. Enl. 2d ed. National Geographic Soc.,
     1966. 343p. $18.75.
     A relatively new and excellent atlas designed to give maxi-
mum information of the kind one seeks in maps. Page-size maps
permit selection of the most desirable map scale for each area.
There are 50 large political maps with some physical features,
plus scenic and historical maps of the United States showing
National Parks and Civil War battlefields. Maps are clear,

attractive, easily read, and descriptive text accompanies each geographical area. Special features are "Great Moments in Geography," "Global Statistics," "Population of Major Cities," and a temperature and rainfall chart for 198 cities around the world. Well indexed.

520 Odyssey world atlas. Odyssey, 1966. 317p. $19.95.

First published in 1966, this new atlas is the work of a panel of ten well-known university geographers. Suitable for students of high school level and up, for adults, and for commercial use. Twenty-one pages of physical, political, and thematic maps of the world in color are followed by maps of the various regions of the world. Contains a comprehensive index. Is notable for its excellent legibility and clarity. Appendix gives capital, largest city, area, and population of countries and regions of the world, world facts and figures, e.g., principal mountains and rivers, largest cities, urbanized areas of the United States, a glossary of geographical terms, a table of foreign language geographical terms, and a list of abbreviations.

521 World book atlas. Field Enterprises, 1966. 392p. $30.45.

First published in 1963, this atlas has been revised and updated annually since then. Designed to complement and supplement the *World Book Encyclopedia* by providing historical, political, relief, and special purpose maps of the world. Arranged in 11 major groupings with 30 percent of map coverage on the United States. There are street maps on important cities in the United States index section. The introduction entitled "How to get the most out of the World Book Atlas" is particularly helpful to high school and college students and adults not familiar with maps and atlases. There is a comprehensive index to the names of 80,000 cities, towns, political units, and geographical features. A list of abbreviations and a glossary giving English equivalents of foreign geographical terms precedes the index. Comprehensive, authoritative, attractive, and easy to use.

522 American Heritage (Periodical). American Heritage pictorial

atlas of U.S. history. McGraw-Hill, 1966. 424p. $16.50.

In the familiar *American Heritage* format, with many panoramas replacing simple maps, this atlas is more colorful and detailed than its predecessors.

523 Heyden, A. A. M. van der, and Scullard, H. H., eds. Atlas of the classical world. Nelson, 1960. 221p. $18.

An excellent atlas of the Graeco-Roman world, with clean, pleasantly colored, easy-to-read maps. Good illustrations. Available also is *The Shorter Atlas of the Classical World,* by the same editors and publisher, 1962. $5.

524 Shepherd, William Robert. Historical atlas. 9th ed. Barnes & Noble, 1964. 115p. $17.50.

This edition contains all the maps of the 8th edition, revised and enlarged, and a special supplement of historical maps for the period 1929–55, prepared by C. S. Hammond & Co.

525 Walsh, S. Padraig, comp. General world atlases in print; a comparative analysis. Bowker, 1966. 66p. Paper $3.

This guide is an aid to selection, based on recommendations of five types of library-accepted reviewing media.

Travel Guides

▶ While there is no travel series currently being published that can compare with the old *Baedekers,* there are many good ones available. Among these are volumes for the continents and for most nations or regions that welcome tourists. A popular compiler of such guides is Eugene Fodor. Travelers have their own favorites, but the Fodor series covers most countries, is inexpensive, and has proved useful for quick reference. Its volumes are published, many annually revised, by McKay, and their prices range from $4.95 to $7.50.

526 Hance, William A. Geography of modern Africa. Columbia Univ. Pr., 1964. 653p. $13.50.

Although this survey is not really up to date, nation by nation, it is excellent for information on natural resources and general regional culture. It indicates promising industrial and economic developments since the end of World War II and the beginning of independence. Includes illustrations, maps, tables, and charts.

527 U.S. Works Progress Administration. State guides.

These volumes were originally issued between 1937 and 1941. Although too few of them have been revised since that time, they continue to be exceedingly useful. Every library should have the guide for its own state, if it is possible to obtain it. Those libraries fortunate enough to have complete sets have an amazing body of well-ordered facts on tap.

528 Wilber, Donald Newton, ed. Nations of Asia. Hart, 1966. 605p. $15.

Signed articles on 24 Asian nations or areas, with pertinent facts stated briefly at conclusion of each chapter. Well illustrated, but most maps are small. Indexed.

529 Wint, Guy. Asia: a handbook. Praeger, 1966. 856p. $25.

Good coverage country by country, followed by essays on religion, art, literature, politics, minorities, world relations, and other aspects of modern world society. An appendix contains postwar treaties and agreements to 1960. Includes small black-and-white maps and a bibliography of American publications. Detailed index.

16
History

United States History

Bibliographies

530 Handlin, Oscar, and others. Harvard guide to American history. Harvard Univ. Pr., 1954. 689p. $12.50; paper $4.95 (Atheneum, 1967).

Interpreting United States history in its broadest aspects, the references continue to be useful for students in spite of the book's publication date.

530a U.S. Library of Congress. General Reference and Bibliography Division. Guide to the study of the United States of America. Govt. Print. Off., 1960. 1193p. $7.

A valuable guide to every phase of American life. Excellent descriptive annotations. Brief biographies of many of the authors included.

Dictionaries and Encyclopedias

531 Boatner, Mark Mayo. Civil War dictionary, a concise encyclopedia. McKay, 1959. 974p. $15.

More than 4000 brief entries, dealing with people, places, military engagements, and special subjects. Maps and diagrams are included. Also contains an atlas of sectional maps covering the Civil War area.

532 ———Encyclopedia of the American Revolution. McKay, 1966. 1287p. $17.50.

Historical interests and activities during the next decade will be increasingly centered on the American Revolution and its bicentenary. This dictionary, which also includes considerable material on events which led to the outbreak of war, should prove a useful first place to look when the questions start to come. Contains a bibliography and short-title index, and an index to maps.

533 Carruth, Gorton, and associates, eds. Encyclopedia of American facts and dates. 4th ed. Crowell, 1966. 821p. $7.95.

Has a chronological arrangement, with parallel columns to show what was happening concurrently in varied fields of endeavor. Specific topics are found through an extensive quick-reference index.

534 Commager, Henry Steele, ed. Documents of American his-

tory. 7th ed. Appleton, 1963. 2v. in 1, 632p., 739p. $8.50. 2v. ed. paper $3.75 each.

The best-known collection of basic documents from 1492 to the present, "designed to illustrate the course of American history from the Age of Discovery to the present [1962]." Arranged chronologically.

535 Concise dictionary of American history. Advisory ed., Thomas C. Cochran; ed., Wayne Andrews. Scribner, 1962. 1156p. $19.50.

This one-volume abridgment of the six-volume *Dictionary of American History* (below) is an excellent concise history, although not a substitute for the complete work. Bibliographies omitted, but there is an excellent index.

536 Dictionary of American history. James Truslow Adams, editor in chief. Scribner [1958]–1961. 6v. and index v. $112 (by subscription only).

Individual entries in all of the volumes are signed, and most of them have a brief bibliography of more extensive works on the subject. Although the subjects appear in alphabetical order, the usefulness of the work is enhanced by numerous cross references and by a good index volume. The first supplement (v.6), which covers the period 1940–60, was edited by J. G. E. Hopkins and Wayne Andrews (1961).

537 Johnson, Thomas Herbert, ed. Oxford companion to American history. Oxford Univ. Pr., 1966. 906p. $12.50.

Almost 5000 entries, including a network of cross references, on significant American people, places, and events.

538 Kane, Joseph Nathan. Famous first facts; a record of first happenings, discoveries, and inventions in the United States. 3d ed. Wilson, 1964. 1165p. $18.

Compilation of first happenings, discoveries, and inventions in America. Several indexes are provided: by years, by days of the month, by personal names, and by geographical location.

539 Mirkin, Stanford M. What happened when. Rev. ed. Washburn, 1966. 442p. $7.95.

A calendar of dates with notable events of each day listed in chronological order by year. Emphasis is on events of the nineteenth and twentieth centuries in the United States, but some others are included.

540 Morris, Richard B. Encyclopedia of American history. Updated and rev. Harper, 1965. 843p. $8.95; lib. bdg. $8.29 net.

Besides the general historical-chronological presentation, there are sections devoted to various special topics: the Constitution and the Supreme Court, thought and culture, American economy, science, and inventions, etc., also presented chronologically. Brief biographies of 400 eminent Americans are included. Maps and charts. Indexed.

Directories

541 American Association for State and Local History. Directory of historical societies and agencies in the United States and Canada, 1967–1968. The Association, 1967. 192p. $3.50.

Libraries should acquire the latest edition of this biennial publication, which lists historical societies geographically, giving mailing address, number of members, museums, hours and size of library, publication program, etc. It is possible to locate societies devoted to a special phase of history through the index.

World History

Bibliographies

542 American Historical Association. Guide to historical literature. Edited by George Frederick Howe and others. Macmillan, 1961. 962p. $16.50.

The best recent guide for general use, and source of many out-of-print titles now being reprinted. Especially valuable for its critical notes. Indexed.

543 American Universities Field Staff. A select bibliography: Asia, Africa, Eastern Europe, Latin America. The Staff, 1960. 534p. $4.75.

——————— ———————Supplements: 1961, paper $1; 1963, paper $1.50; 1965, paper $2.

An annotated list of approximately 7000 books and journals. Most are in English, some in other Western languages; full bibliographic information is provided. Broad in scope and not limited to political or social studies, although these predominate. Anthropology, language and literature, art, etc. are also covered. Author and title indexes.

General World History

544 Breasted, James H. Conquest of civilization. New ed. edited by Edith Williams Ware. Harper, 1954. 669p. $8.95.

A standard work and a good general introduction to the cultures of the ancient world. Designed for consecutive reading, the book has reference value in its detailed index. Recent archaeological advances in Near East studies may cause its days to be numbered, but Breasted's writing is itself based on many years of thorough archaeological investigation by himself and his colleagues. Illustrations, maps.

545 Collison, Robert, comp. Dictionary of dates and anniversaries. Transatlantic Arts, 1967. 428p. $8.75.

Part I is in alphabetical order by name of person, place, or event—very brief information, serving merely to identify and establish dates. Selective, with British emphasis, but covering events back to B.C. all over the world. Part II refers to the same events in calendar order.

546 Hayes, Carlton J. H., and others. History of Western civilization. Macmillan, 1962. 919p. $9.95. 2v. ed. $7.95 each.

A good outline history, from the ancient Near East to the present day. Includes brief consideration of literary-artistic movements as well as political-military events. Illustrations. Adequate index. Appendix contains a select list of European sovereigns.

547 Langer, William Leonard. Encyclopedia of world history: ancient, medieval and modern, chronologically arranged. Rev. 3d ed. Houghton, 1952. 1243p. $12.50. (4th ed. rev. and enl. in prep.)

Events of world history concisely presented in an arrangement that is first geographical and then chronological. Maps and genealogical tables. Appendixes list rulers, i.e., Roman emperors; Roman Catholic popes; British, French, and Italian ministries; and United States presidents. Indexed.

548 Swain, Joseph W. Ancient world. Harper, 1950. 2v. $7.75 each.

This history of man from prehistoric times to the fall of Rome contains much opinion, but the viewpoints are based on serious scholarship. Basically a sophisticated text for consecutive reading, but frequent charts and tables have factual reference value. Illustrations, maps, bibliography, and index for each volume.

549 Viorst, Milton, ed. Great documents of Western civilization. Chilton, 1965. 388p. $7.95.

The most inclusive book of sources from the rise of Christianity to United Nations Charter available in one volume. Contains a reading list and an index.

550 Worldmark encyclopedia of the nations. Ed. and publisher, Moshe Y. Sachs. 3d rev. ed. Harper, 1967. 5v. $59.95.

Articles on each nation of the world, with data in uniform order. Some illustrations and small maps. This edition revised for statistics and government changes through 1965. Seven new African nations have been added since the 1963 edition.

European History

551 Black, Cyril E., and Helmreich, E. C. Twentieth century Europe. 3d rev. ed. Knopf, 1966. 939p. $13.75.

An authoritative survey of modern Europe, especially valuable for its extensive coverage of Eastern Europe. Other areas, such as Africa, are also treated if they have had an effect on Europe. Good appendixes, including a section on postwar pacts and a twentieth-century chronology. Illustrations, maps, and extensive bibliography; good index.

552 Davis, William S. Life on a medieval barony. Harper, 1951. 414p. $5; lib. bdg. $4.43 net.

The elaborate narrative style of this book does not diminish its reference value because of its good organization, exhaustive detail, and adequate indexing. Well illustrated and authoritative; generally considered the best one-volume work in English on everyday life in the Middle Ages. Illustrated. Indexed. Originally published in the 1920's.

553 Ergang, Robert R. Europe from the Renaissance to Waterloo. 3d ed. Heath, 1967. 753p. $8.95.

544 ———Europe since Waterloo. 3d. ed. Heath, 1967. 952p. $9.50.

555 ———Europe in our time; 1914 to the present. 3d ed. Heath, 1958. 973p. $9.

These three volumes provide a chronological survey of the economic, political, and social history of Europe. Extensive bibliographies in each volume. Well indexed.

556 Falls, Cyril. Great war: 1914–1918. Putnam, 1959. 447p. $6.95; paper $1.95.

A standard history of World War I, by Britain's official historian of that conflict. Emphasizes the military, but written in exciting narrative style. Illustrations, portraits, and maps. Includes a brief bibliography and an index of names and places.

557 Snyder, Louis L. The war; a concise history, 1939–1945. Simon & Schuster, 1960. 579p. $7.95; paper $.95 (Dell).

A one-volume summary of World War II, containing all the important facts, dates, and names involved. The style is journalistic, but the facts are accurate. Illustrations, portraits, maps.

Adequate bibliography and index. Appendixes include headline history of World War II, a selected list of World War II military code names, and a glossary on major conferences of World War II.

558 Stearns, Raymond P. Pageant of Europe; sources and selections from the Renaissance to the present day. Rev. ed. Harcourt, 1961. 1072p. $11.75; paper $5.50.

Intended as supplementary material for use in college survey courses. Arrangement is topical, then chronological. The source materials are excerpted and are accompanied by interpretive background. Documents are selected for their reliability, their readability, and their high degree of impact on the ideas, events, or people of their time. Sources are cited. Indexed.

559 Stephenson, Carl. Mediaeval history; Europe from the second to the sixteenth century. Edited and rev. by Bryce Lyon. 4th ed. Harper, 1962. 639p. $9.25.

First published in 1935, this latest edition of a work intended primarily for college students has been revised by Bryce Lyon. Covers political, cultural, social, and economic history. Quotations from contemporary documents included in the text. Chapter bibliographies, genealogical tables, and chronological charts. Illustrated and indexed.

European History by Country

England

560 Lunt, William E. History of England. 4th ed. Harper, 1957. 980p. $9.75.

A political history from the beginning through 1955, useful for brief information about important persons, events, or periods in English history. Maps, chronological tables, a 66-page bibliography, and a fairly detailed index.

561 Trevelyan, George M. Illustrated English social history. Illus-

trations selected by Ruth C. Wright. McKay, 1949–52. 4v. $8.50 each. Published in 1942 under title: English social history.

Contents: v.1, Chaucer's England and the early Tudors; v.2, The age of Shakespeare and the Stuart period; v.3, The eighteenth century; v.4, The nineteenth century.

Carefully chosen and pertinent illustrations accompany a concise and brilliant text describing scenes from daily life. Illustrations well reproduced and usually from contemporary English sources, which are provided. Each volume is separately indexed.

France

562 Guerard, Albert L. France; a modern history. Univ. of Michigan Pr., 1959. 563p. $8.75.

A good concise history, written in a lively manner. Though the book is part of the University of Michigan's "History of the Modern World" series, the first 200 pages deal with early France. Bibliography; well indexed.

Germany

563 Flenley, Ralph. Modern German history. 2d rev. ed. Dutton, 1964. 491p. $7.50.

An excellent one-volume history, covering the period from the Reformation to the present. The text strikes an admirable balance between conciseness and completeness. Good on cultural and literary trends. Contains illustrations, maps, select bibliography, and an index to places and names.

Italy

564 Mack Smith, Denis. Italy; modern history. Univ. of Michigan Pr., 1959. 508p. $7.50.

A standard survey in English of Italian history from the unification to the present. Author's personal stamp is evident, but the work has been well received by all reviewers. Bibliography and a good index.

Russia and the Soviet Union

565 Horecky, Paul L., ed. Russia and the Soviet Union; a bibliographic guide to Western-language publications. Univ. of Chicago Pr., 1965. 473p. $8.95.

"... A conspectus of those Western-language writings, chiefly
in book form, . . . particularly relevant to the study of the
political, socio-economic, and intellectual life. . . ."—*Introduction.* Arranged by broad topics, this work covers approximately
2000 titles selected for their relevance and recency. Excellent
annotations and good indexing. Bibliographic citations are un-
cluttered, providing sufficient information for identification.

566 Pares, *Sir* Bernard. A history of Russia. Knopf, 1953. 611p.
$8; paper $2.95 (Vintage).

This remains the best one-volume history in English of
Russia and of the Soviet Union. An exceptionally detailed index
and a comprehensive bibliography make this a useful reference
tool. Includes maps.

567 Utechin, Sergej. Everyman's concise encyclopaedia of Russia.
Dutton, 1961. 623p. $6.50; paper $2.65.

An excellent, short-article encyclopedia of "contemporary
Russia and its historical background," people, places, and
things. An admirable supplement to Pares. Illustrations and
portraits. Contains a Systematic List of Entries to related
subjects.

568 Walsh, Warren B. Russia and the Soviet Union; a modern
history. Univ. of Michigan Pr., 1958. 640p. $10.

A handy, one-volume work, useful especially for the modern
era, but should be considered only as a supplement to Pares.
Illustrations and maps. Reviewers found gaps but felt this was,
on the whole, an intelligent treatment, especially of recent
events. Bibliography.

Spain

569 Altamira y Crevea, Rafael. History of Spain from the begin-

nings to the present day. Trans. by Muna Lee. Van Nostrand, 1949. 748p. $9.75.

A manual based on (but not an abridgment of) the author's four-volume history, which appeared early in this century. Detailed treatment, with useful appendix material, including tables of dates of events, of developments in the arts, inventions, etc. Illustrations, portraits, and maps. The bibliography is mainly of works in English. Because of the author's objectivity and the book's careful indexing, this Spanish history is more easily used as a reference tool than Madariaga's work which follows.

570 Madariaga, Salvador de. Spain; a modern history. Praeger, 1958. 736p. $8.50.

The sometimes controversial but always brilliant interpreter of Spain here emphasizes the events leading to the Civil War, although the book begins with prehistory. Not a listing of events, but a presentation of the author's feeling for his country. He is most objective when treating the pre-Franco period. Because of the author's personal involvement, this work is less useful as a day-to-day reference tool than as a highly important contribution to the literature of Spanish history. This edition, based on the author's work originally published in 1930, has additional material. Indexed, but no bibliography.

Asian and Middle Eastern History

571 Buss, Claude A. Asia in the modern world; a history of China, Japan, South and Southeast Asia. Macmillan, 1964. 767p. $8.95.

A good general summary of modern Asia's relationship with Western countries. The book's reference value lies in its being a summarized history of these several countries—emphasizing their individual and collective interaction—between the covers of one volume. Moderately complete index, a brief bibliography, and maps.

572 Fisher, Sydney N. Middle East; a history. Knopf, 1959. 650p. $11.25.

This history begins with the rise of Islam and continues, with a substantial section on the twentieth century, to the present. A good index enhances the reference value of this work, which is limited in scope but of particular importance in Turkish studies, the author's specialty. Contains maps, and a bibliography at end of each chapter.

573 Sachar, Abram L. A history of the Jews. 5th rev. ed. Knopf, 1964. 478p. $7.95; paper $2.95.

A good summary with an adequate index. Latest edition does not update early sections on the patriarchs and prophets, but, beginning with David, the book is on surer ground and brings the story up to the present day. Brief bibliography. Indexed.

African History

574 Legum, Colin, ed. Africa; a handbook to the continent. Rev. and enl. ed. Praeger, 1966. 558p. $18.50.

Because of the nature of Africa today, no book is really up to date, but this is a most useful one-volume reference work on African affairs. One section deals with each nation; a second section treats the continent as a whole. An authoritative book, each chapter by a specialist. Illustrations and maps. Carefully indexed.

Latin-American History

575 Humphreys, Robin Arthur. Latin American history, a guide to the literature in English. Oxford Univ. Pr., 1958. 197p. $4.

Issued under the auspices of the Royal Institute of International Affairs. This can serve as a companion volume to the *Harvard Guide to American History,* as it does for the history of Latin America what the *Harvard Guide* does for United States history.

576 Munro, Dana Gardner. Latin American republics: a history. 3d ed. Appleton, 1960. 547p. $6.75.

Since there is no one-volume reference book available on the history of Latin America, the Martin and Lovett *Encyclopedia of Latin-American History* being out of print, Munro's history is suggested as a reference source. There are many other titles in the field, including the two-volume *History of the Americas* by John Francis Bannon (2d ed. McGraw-Hill, 1963) and *A History of the Americas,* also in two volumes, by Vera Brown Holmes (Ronald, 1950–64).

Canadian History

577 Encyclopedia Canadiana. Grolier, 1965. 10v. $99.50.
    Very thorough coverage of Canadian life in all its aspects—political, biographical, geographical, historical—with good material on labor and industry, social sciences, and Canadian flora and fauna. Particularly recommended for those states bordering on Canada. Volume 10 contains an atlas with an index to the atlas. No general index to the set.

17
Biography, Genealogy, and Names

Indexes

578 Biography index; a cumulative index to biographical material in books and magazines. Jan. 1946– . Wilson, 1947– . Quarterly (Nov., Feb., May, Aug.) with annual and permanent three-year cumulations. $20 a year. v.1–6 (1946–64) available at $40 each.
    Indexes biographical articles published after 1946 in approximately 1600 periodicals, current books of individual and collected biography, obituaries, and incidental biographical material in otherwise nonbiographical books. Index includes main or "name" alphabet and an index by professions and occupations.

General Biography

579 Current biography. Monthly (except Aug.); cumulated annually. Wilson, 1940– . Annual subscription $6.

Biographical sketches of newsworthy individuals of various nationalities with bibliographies and portraits. Indexes cumulate. Annual volumes, 1946 to date, are available at $7 each, and are not part of the subscription. Cumulated Index to *Current Biography,* 1951–60, 1961–65 free. Small libraries may find annual volumes sufficient.

580 Delaney, John J., and Tobin, James Edward. Dictionary of Catholic biography. Doubleday, 1961. 1245p. $7.49.

More than 13,000 brief biographies of saints, popes, church fathers, and Catholic laymen. Appendixes include the saints as patrons of groups of people and of places, a list of symbols of saints in art, and a chronological chart of popes and world rulers.

581 Dictionary of American biography. Scribner, 1957. 11v. $264 (by subscription only).

The standard reference for biography of important Americans who died before 1941. Each article documented with primary sources whenever possible. Each volume of this edition contains two of the original. Volume 11 contains the two supplements, bringing coverage up through 1940.

582 Concise dictionary of American biography. Scribner, 1964 1273p. $22.50.

An excellent condensation of the *Dictionary of American Biography,* including only Americans who died before 1941.

583 Dictionary of Canadian biography. Edited by George W. Brown, Marcel Trudel and André Vachon. Univ. of Toronto Pr., 1966–   . v.1. $15.

The first volume of this national biographical dictionary, covering the period 1000–1700, contains 594 biographies and a series of historical essays of importance for the United States as well as Canada. Bibliography at end of each article and a general bibliography and index at end of the volume. A French-language edition is published by Les Presses de l'Université Laval, Quebec.

584 Dictionary of national biography. Edited by *Sir* Leslie Stephen and *Sir* Sidney Lee. Oxford Univ. Pr., 1882–1949. 1953. 22v. and suppl.1, $208; suppl.2, $16.80; suppl.3 and 4, $10.10 each; suppl.5, $11.20; suppl.6, $19.20.

Well-documented and signed biographies of notable inhabitants of the British Isles who died before 1950. Bibliography included for each biography.

585 ————Concise dictionary. Oxford Univ. Pr., 1961. 2v. $17.60; v.1 $10.40, v.2 $7.20.

A condensation and an index of the parent set; includes brief biographies of more than 30,000 notable inhabitants of the British Isles who died before 1950.

586 Durant, John, and Durant, Alice. Pictorial history of American presidents. 4th rev. ed. Barnes, 1965. 356p. $7.95.

This revision, covering Presidents from Washington to Lyndon B. Johnson, is a photograph album with running text explaining the pictures. Gives additional information when events were dramatic, amusing, or far-reaching in historical effect.

587 Kane, Joseph Nathan. Facts about the presidents. Wilson, 1959. 348p. $6 (out of print); paper $.75 (Pocket Bks.).

Chapters on each President, in chronological order, are followed by charts and tables of miscellaneous comparative data. Includes portraits and facsimile autographs. New edition announced for 1968.

588 New century cyclopedia of names. Appleton, 1954. 3v. $39.50.

Essential facts for more than 100,000 proper names of every description—persons, places, historical events, plays, operas, works of fiction, literary characters, mythological and legendary persons, etc. Volume 3 contains chronological table of world history, rulers and popes, genealogical charts, and prenames with pronunciation.

589 U.S. Congress Biographical directory of the American Con-

gress, 1774–1961. Govt. Print. Off., 1961. 1863p. $11.75.

Lists executive officers, and gives biographies of members of Congress from the first through the eighty-sixth congresses.

590 Webster's Biographical dictionary. Merriam, 1964. 1697p. $8.50.

Useful for quick reference. Information given is necessarily brief, as more than 40,000 names are included. Pronunciation, dates, and chief contribution to civilization are given. Appended are a pronouncing list of "prenames" and some tables of Presidents, sovereigns, members of the Hall of Fame, and the like.

591   Who's who. Annual. St. Martin's, 1849– . 1966/67 $27.50; 1967/68 $30.

Emphasis is on who's who in Britain, but notables of other countries are included. Small libraries may purchase at intervals of several years without losing major value.

592 Who's who in America. Biennial. Marquis, 1889– . 1966/ 67 $32.50.

Abbreviated biographical information. This series, combined with *Who Was Who in America* and the *Historical Volume,* gives quick-reference access to facts about prominent persons in the United States from 1607 to the present.

593 Who was who in America. Marquis. 4v. Historical volume, 1607–1896, 672p.; v.1, 1897–1942, 1408p.; v.2, 1943–50, 614p.; v.3, 1951–60, 959p. $26 each.

These four volumes, plus the contemporary volume *Who's Who in America,* constitute the series *Who's Who in American History.* Chief use of the four historical volumes is for identification of people who were once prominent, whether or not their fame lived after them.

Artists

594 Bénézit, Emmanuel. Dictionnaire critique et documentaire des peintres, sculpteurs, dessinateurs et graveurs, nouv. éd.

Paris, Gründ [1956–61; c1948–55] (available Boston Book and Art Shop, Inc.). 8v. $160.

A comprehensive work covering Eastern and Western art, including many minor artists from earliest times to 1947 for Volume 1, and into the 1950's for Volume 8. Reproduces symbols and signatures of the artists and lists chief works and where found.

595 Cummings, Paul. A dictionary of contemporary American artists. St. Martin's, 1966. 331p. $17.50.

Professional information about 697 American artists of the last 25 years who are represented in permanent collections. Information concise. Includes also birth dates and name pronunciations where deemed necessary. Illustrated. Contains bibliography.

596 Fielding, Mantle. Dictionary of American painters, sculptors and engravers. With an Addendum containing corrections and additional material on the original entries. James F. Carr, 1965. 488p. $28.50.

Reprint of the work published in 1926 with an addendum compiled by the publisher, including many new names. Brief biographies of nearly 10,000 artists.

597 Who's who in American art. Bowker. Triennial. $22.50 in 1966 ($20 to AFA members).

At head of title: The American Federation of Arts. Edited by Dorothy B. Gilbert. Previously part of the *American Art Annual*. Includes Canadian biographies, a geographical index, obituaries 1963–66, and a list of open exhibitions arranged geographically.

Authors and Writers

598 Contemporary authors, a bio-bibliographical guide to current authors and their works. Semiannual. Gale Res., 1962–   . Annual subscription $25.

Originally published quarterly. Volume 4 (fall 1963) and

subsequent volumes double numbered to indicate they are equivalent to two quarterly volumes. Current volume is 19/20 (1968). Articles are brief and factual, listing all works published for a large number of authors hard to find in other sources. Each volume has a cumulated index for all previous volumes.

599 Kunitz, Stanley J., and Haycraft, Howard, eds. American authors, 1600–1900. Wilson, 1938. 846p. $8.
   Biographies are written in an easy style. Brief bibliographies and portraits included.

600 ———British authors before 1800. Wilson, 1952. 584p. $8.

601 ———British authors of the 19th century. Wilson, 1936. 677p. $8.
   Companion volumes for biographical sketches of most British authors prior to 1900. Bibliographies and portraits.

602 ———Junior book of authors. 2d ed. rev. Wilson, 1951. 309p. $6.
   Provides basic reference for biographical information about 289 authors of children's books, current and past.

603 Fuller, Muriel, ed. More junior authors. Wilson, 1963. 235p. $6.
   Supplements *Junior Book of Authors,* by Stanley J. Kunitz and Howard Haycraft (above). Provides biographies of 268 authors and illustrators of children's books not included in the original work.

604 Kunitz, Stanley J., and Haycraft, Howard, eds. Twentieth century authors. Wilson, 1942. 1577p. $15. 1st supplement, edited by Stanley J. Kunitz and Vineta Colby, 1955. 1123p. $12.
   Biographies of the best-known world authors of the twentieth century. Short articles, each with a portrait and bibliography.

605 Kunitz, Stanley J., and Colby, Vineta, eds. European authors, 1000–1900. Wilson, 1967. 1016p. $18.

In the same format and style as the other books in Wilson's "Authors Series"; covers 967 writers of 31 different continental European literatures, including Hebrew.

606 Magill, Frank N., ed. Cyclopedia of world authors. Harper, 1958. 1198p. $10.95; lib. bdg. $8.97 net.

Biographical details and critical and literary evaluations of 793 authors whose works are listed in Magill's *Masterpieces of World Literature*. Major works with dates. Bibliographic references are given at the end of each entry.

607 Untermeyer, Louis. Lives of the poets: the story of 1000 years of English and American poetry. Simon & Schuster, 1959. 757p. $7.95; paper $2.95.

From Chaucer to Dylan Thomas. Well indexed.

Music

608 Baker, Theodore. Baker's Biographical dictionary of musicians. 5th ed. rev. by Nicholas Slonimsky. Schirmer, 1958, with 1965 supplement. 1855p., 143p. $25; supplement only, $5.

Very brief articles about composers, performers, critics, conductors, and teachers, arranged alphabetically under surname with pronunciation. Bibliographies included.

609 Ewen, David. Great composers, 1300–1900; a biographical and critical guide. Wilson, 1966. 429p. $10.

List of principal works and works about each composer accompany the biographies. Portraits. Appendixes contain chronological and geographical lists. Supersedes the author's *Composers of Yesterday* (1937).

610 ———Living musicians. Wilson, 1940. 390p. $5. Supplement, 1957. 178p. $4.

Although old, still suitable for general reference use since it includes portraits and bibliographical references and can be supplemented by *Current Biography*. Both volumes contain a classified list of musicians.

611 ———New book of modern composers. 3d ed. rev. and enl. Knopf, 1961. 491p. $7.95.

Similar in format to the author's *World of Great Composers from Palestrina to Debussy,* this volume provides a cross section of the music of the past 50 years through presentation of 32 composers.

612 ———Popular American composers from Revolutionary times to the present. Wilson, 1962. 217p. $7.

Brief, readable articles on about 130 composers. The title index of their compositions is worthy of mention. Contains a chronological list of popular American composers. Portraits.

613 ———World of great composers from Palestrina to Debussy. Prentice-Hall, 1962. 576p. $15.

37 composers are discussed from four points of view: factual biography, the composer as seen by a contemporary, as seen by the modern music world, and as seen by himself. Includes bibliographical appendixes and a detailed index.

Religion

614 Book of saints. Compiled by Benedictine monks of St. Augustine's Abbey, Ramsgate. 5th ed. Crowell, 1966. 740p. $8.95.

A new edition of a standard biographical dictionary of saints, including many lesser-known English ones and some recently canonized, who are not included in Butler's *Lives of the Saints.*

615 Butler, Alban. Lives of the saints. Edited by Herbert Thurston and D. Attwater. Kenedy, 1956. 4v. $39.50; paper $1.95 (Benziger).

The standard reference work for students and adults.

616 Moyer, Elgin S. Who was who in church history. Rev. ed. Moody Press, 1967. 452p. $6.95.

A brief biographical dictionary of distinguished leaders of the Christian church, including Catholics, Protestants, Gnostics, Mormons, Quakers, Spiritualists, etc. A foreword suggests other more extensive sources of this type of information.

Science

617 American men of science, physical and biological sciences. 11th ed. Bowker, 1965–67. 6v. $25 each. Suppl.1, Summer 1966, paper $10; Suppl.2, Fall 1966, $15; Suppl.3, Spring 1967, paper $15; Suppl.4, Fall 1967, $20; set of 4 suppl., $50.
Biographies of more than 100,000 scientists.

618 Asimov, Isaac. Asimov's Biographical encyclopedia of science and technology. Doubleday, 1964. 662p. $8.95.
The nonalphabetical arrangement of biographies is designed to show the influence of outstanding scientists upon their followers. Useful for most school assignments and adult nonspecialists. Indexed.

619 McGraw-Hill Encyclopedia of Science and Technology. Modern men of science. McGraw-Hill, 1966. 620p. $19.50.
Sketches of 426 contemporary scientists who have been winners of major prizes in science since 1940. Each article includes a portrait and about a page of text, with a reference to the article in the *Encyclopedia* where more information may be found. The two-part analytical index provides a means of finding a person or a subject in any part of the volume, and gives a classified listing of the biographical articles by subject fields.

Theater Arts

620 Biographical encyclopedia and who's who of the American theatre. Edited by Walter Rigdon. Heinemann, 1966. 1101p. $82.50.
In spite of its price, this is a worthwhile purchase for a library of any size. Contents: New York productions (alphabetical by title) presented from 1900 through May 31, 1964; complete

playbills since 1959 for New York City and leading experimental and repertory theater groups of the United States; premieres abroad of American plays since 1946; complete biographies of most important living persons connected with each aspect of the American theater; biographies of American theater groups, existing and extinct, including production records; histories of New York theater buildings; record of major awards; a biographical bibliography; discography of original-cast recordings; and necrology.

621 Who's who in the theatre; a biographical record of the contemporary stage. Edited by Freda Gaye. 14th ed. Pitman, 1967. 1720p. $25.

While the British stage is emphasized, the biographical section includes many Americans, from George Abbott to Blanche Yurka. This Jubilee edition contains encyclopedic information on the London stage and a little on the New York one. Contains index of London playbills, Shakespeare playbills, notable productions and long runs, obituaries, etc.

Genealogy and Names

622 Doane, Gilbert Harry. Searching for your ancestors. 3d rev. ed. Univ. of Minnesota Pr., 1960. 198p. $3.95.

A general discussion of how to pursue the study and practice of family history, and how to record the information when it is found. Its reference value is in its bibliography, its information on United States census records and state vital statistics, and its finding list of sources to search for records of soldiers of the American Revolution.

623 Shankle, George Earlie. American nicknames: their origin and significance. 2d ed. Wilson, 1955. 524p. $7.50.

Covers a wide range of subjects: the sobriquets and appellations of persons, places, objects, and events in American life, past and present. Bibliographical footnotes.

624 Smith, Elsdon D. Dictionary of American family names. Harper, 1956. 244p. $4.95.

Gives derivations of more than 6000 family names, with variant spellings. The most cosmopolitan of the surname dictionaries, but the ascribed meanings are not documented.

625 Stevenson, Noel C. Search and research, the researcher's handbook. Deseret, 1964. 364p. $2.95.

A guide to the location of vital records in the United States, Canada, and throughout the world. Useful handbook not only for the genealogist (to whom it is primarily addressed), but also for the historian, lawyer, and librarian. L. G. Pine's *American Origins* (Doubleday, 1960), which offers excellent guidance to genealogical records outside the United States and Great Britain, is to be reissued by the Genealogical Book Co. in 1967.

Heraldry, Flags, and Decorations

626 Adam, Frank. Clans, septs, and regiments of the Scottish highlands . . . Rev. by *Sir* Thomas Innes of Learney. 4th ed. Johnston, 1952. 624p. 55s.

A reliable guide to the problems raised by Scottish tartans, together with information on clans, septs, and military organizations.

627 Boutell, Charles. Boutell's Heraldry. Rev. by C. W. Scott-Giles and J. P. Brooke-Little. Warne, 1966. 329p. $12.50.

Since the first edition of 1863, this book has gone through many revisions. It is now generally regarded as the standard work of reference on heraldry, although the viewpoint is primarily British.

628 Campbell, *Vice-Admiral* Gordon, and Evans, I. O. Book of flags. 5th ed. Oxford Univ. Pr., 1965. 124p. $5.

A useful book, brought up to date by Mr. Evans. The illustrations are in color, or are drawn with hatching when in black and white. The book is especially rich in emblems of the British Commonwealth, and is excellent in its material on such flags as those of the African republics which became independent states after 1957.

629 Dorling, Henry Taprell. Ribbons and medals, naval, military, air force and civil. Philip, 1963. 301p. 25s.

This new edition, a second impression with enlarged supplement, was prepared in association with L. F. Guille. The ribbons, given for most of the world, are illustrated in color. The medals are described, their origin and purpose are given, and in many cases the entry is accompanied by an illustration.

630 Flags of the world. Rev. by E. M. C. Barraclough. Warne, 1965. 325p. $10.

Earlier editions of this well-known work were signed by F. E. Hulme (1897) and H. Gresham Carr (1953). The latest edition has illustrations of 340 flags in color and 400 text drawings in black and white. Although especially strong for the British Commonwealth, the book attempts to cover the entire world.

631 Kerrigan, Evans E. American war medals and decorations. Viking, 1964. 149p. $6.50.

Contains information and illustrations of decorations of honor and service medals given to personnel of the United States armed services, together with wartime awards given to civilians. Contains chronological table of awards with authorization. Bibliography. Indexed. Illustrated.

632 Stewart, George R. Names on the land, a historical account of place-naming in the United States. Rev. and enl. ed. Houghton, 1958. 511p. $6.

The index to this book on place-names leads to a wide variety of facts on the origin of the names of towns, cities, and geographical features in the United States. Illustrated. Includes bibliography.

633 U.S. Immigration and Naturalization Service. Foreign ver-

sions of English names. Rev. Govt. Print. Off., 1962. Unpaged. $.30.

This Publication M-131 of the U.S. Immigration and Naturalization Service is a catalog of charts "designed to aid the person who needs to know the equivalent of commonly used English given names." Some names are given in as many as 16 languages.

634 Wells, Evelyn. What to name the baby. Doubleday, 1953. 326p. $2.95.

The original title of this work was *A Treasury of Names*. It was compiled by a scholar, and although she gives no sources, the book has always been especially helpful in giving variants and foreign equivalents of first names. Since styles in naming new babies change rather quickly, many libraries will wish to supplement this book with *Book of Girls' Names* and *Book of Boys' Names,* both by Linwood Sleigh and Charles Johnson, and both published in 1963 by Thomas Y. Crowell, at $4.50 each.

Directory of Publishers

Abingdon. Abingdon Press, 201 Eighth Ave. S., Nashville, Tenn. 37202

Abrams. Harry N. Abrams, Inc., 6 West 57th St., New York, N.Y. 10019

Adrian. Adrian Press, 550 Fifth Ave., New York, N.Y. 10036

Aldine. Aldine Publishing Co., 320 West Adams St., Chicago, Ill. 60606

Am. Hospital Assn. American Hospital Assn., 840 North Lake Shore Dr., Chicago, Ill. 60611

Am. Radio. American Radio Relay League, Inc., 225 Main St., Newington, Conn. 06111

American Association for State and Local History. 132 Ninth Ave. N., Nashville, Tenn. 37203

American Council on Education. 1785 Massachusetts Ave., Washington, D.C. 20006

American Foundation for the Blind, Inc. 15 West 16th St., New York, N.Y. 10011

American Library Assn. Publishing Dept., 50 East Huron St., Chicago, Ill. 60611

American Public Welfare Assn. 1313 East 60th St., Chicago, Ill. 60637

American Register of Exporters and Importers Corp., Inc. 90 West Broadway, New York, N.Y. 10007

American Universities Field Staff, Inc. 366 Madison Ave., New York, N.Y. 10017

Appleton. Appleton-Century-Crofts: refer orders for trade books to: 1716 Locust St., Des Moines, Ia. 50309

Atheneum. Atheneum Publishers, 122 East 42d St., New York, N.Y. 10017

Ayer. N. W. Ayer & Son, Inc., West Washington Sq., Philadelphia, Pa. 19106

Baker Book House. 1019 Wealthy St. S.E., Grand Rapids, Mich. 49506

Bankers Pub. Bankers Publishing Co., 89 Beach St., Boston, Mass. 02111

Banta. George Banta Publishing Co., Curtis Reed Plaza, Menasha, Wis. 54952

Barnes. A. S. Barnes & Co., Inc., Forsgate Dr., Cranbury, N.J. 08512

Barnes & Noble. Barnes & Noble, Inc., 105 Fifth Ave., New York, N.Y. 10003

Beacon. Beacon Press, 25 Beacon St., Boston, Mass. 02108

Bedminster Pr. The Bedminster Press, Vreeland Ave., Totowa, N.J. 07512

Bellman. Bellman Publishing Co., Box 172, Cambridge, Mass. 02138

Bellwether Publishing Co. 167 East 67th St., New York, N.Y. 10021

Benziger. Benziger Publishing Co.,

7 East 51st St., New York, N.Y. 10022

Best. Alfred M. Best Co., Inc., Columbia Rd. and Park Ave., Morristown, N.J. 07960

Blaisdell Pub. Blaisdell Publishing Co., 275 Wyman St., Waltham, Mass. 02154

Bobbs. Bobbs-Merrill Co., Inc., 4300 West 62d St., Indianapolis, Ind. 46206

Books. Books, Inc., 432 Park Ave. S., New York, N.Y. 10016

Borden. Borden Publishing Co., 1855 West Main St., Alhambra, Calif. 91801

Boston Book and Art Shop, Inc. 657 Boylston St., Boston, Mass. 02116

Bowker. R. R. Bowker Co., 1180 Avenue of the Americas, New York, N.Y. 10036

Branford. Charles T. Branford Co., 28 Union St., Newton Centre, Mass. 02159

Braziller. George Braziller, Inc.: refer orders to: Simon & Schuster, Inc., 1 West 39th St., New York, N.Y. 10018

Bruce. Bruce Publishing Co., 400 North Broadway, Milwaukee, Wis. 53201

Burke's Peerage. Burke's Peerage, Ltd., Mercury House, 109–19 Waterloo Rd., London, S.E.1, England

Butterworth & Co. Butterworth & Co., Ltd., 88 Kingsway, London, W.C.2, England

Cambridge Univ. Pr. Cambridge University Press: refer orders to: 510 North Ave., New Rochelle, N.Y. 10801

Carnegie Lib., Pittsburgh. Carnegie Library, 4400 Forbes Ave., Pittsburgh, Pa. 15213

Century House. Watkins Glen, N.Y. 14891

Chemical Pub. Co. Chemical Publishing Co., Inc.: refer trade orders to: Tudor Publishing Co., 221 Park Ave. S., New York, N.Y. 10003

Chemical Rubber Co. 18901 Cranwood Pkwy., Cleveland, O. 44128

Chilton. Chilton Books, 401 Walnut St., Philadelphia, Pa. 19106

Citadel. Citadel Press, Inc., 222 Park Ave. S., New York, N.Y. 10003

Collier-Macmillan Library Service. See Macmillan.

Columbia Univ. Pr. Columbia University Press, 440 West 110th St., New York, N.Y. 10025

Commodity Research Bureau. 82 Beaver St., New York, N.Y. 10005

Cooper Sq. Cooper Square Publishers, Inc., 59 Fourth Ave., New York. N.Y. 10003

Copp. The Copp Clark Publishing Co., Ltd., 517 Wellington St. W., Toronto 2B, Ont., Canada

Cornell Univ. Pr. Cornell University Press, 124 Roberts Pl., Ithaca, N.Y. 14850

Council of State Governments. 1313 East 60th St., Chicago, Ill. 60637

Council on Foreign Relations, Inc. 58 East 68th St., New York, N.Y. 10021

Croner Pub. Croner Publications, Ltd., 211–03 Jamaica Ave., Queens Village, N.Y. 11429

Crowell. Thomas Y. Crowell Co., 201 Park Ave. S., New York, N.Y. 10003

Crown. Crown Publishers, Inc., 419 Park Ave. S., New York, N.Y. 10016

Dartnell Corp. The Dartnell Corp., 4660 Ravenswood Ave., Chicago, Ill. 60640

Day. The John Day Co., Inc.: refer orders to: 200 Madison Ave., New York, N.Y. 10016.

Dell. Dell Publishing Co., 750 Third Ave., New York, N.Y. 10017

Deseret. Deseret Book Co., 44 East South Temple St., Box 958, Salt Lake City, Utah 84111

Dodd. Dodd, Mead & Company, Inc., 79 Madison Ave., New York, N.Y. 10016

Doubleday. Doubleday & Co., Inc.: refer orders to: 501 Franklin Ave., Garden City, N.Y. 11530

Dover. Dover Publications, Inc., 180 Varick St., New York, N.Y. 10014

Duell. Duell, Sloan & Pearce, Inc.: refer orders to: Meredith Press, 1716 Locust St., Des Moines, Ia. 50303

Dufour. Dufour Editions, Chester Springs, Pa. 19425

Dun & Bradstreet. Dun & Bradstreet Publications Corp., 99 Church St., New York, N.Y. 10007

Dutton. E. P. Dutton & Co., Inc., 201 Park Ave. S., New York, N.Y. 10003

Editor and Publisher. Editor and Publisher Co., Inc., 850 Third Ave., New York, N.Y. 10022

Editorial Espasa Calpe. Calle de Felipe IV, Madrid, Spain

Educational Directories, Inc. P.O. Box 199, Mount Prospect, Ill. 60056

Educational Testing Service. 20 Nassau St., Princeton, N.J. 08540

Educators Progress Service. Box 497, Randolph, Wis. 53956

Encyclopaedia Britannica. Encyclopaedia Britannica, Inc., 425 N. Michigan Ave., Chicago, Ill. 60611

Faber. Faber and Faber, Ltd., 24 Russell Sq., London, W.C.1, England

Farrar, Straus. Farrar, Straus & Giroux, Inc., 19 Union Sq. W., New York, N.Y. 10003

Faxon. F. W. Faxon Co., 515–25 Hyde Park Ave., Boston, Mass. 02131

Federation of American Societies for Experimental Biology. 9650 Rockville Pike, Bethesda, Md. 20014

Field Enterprises. Field Enterprises Educational Corp., 510 Merchandise Mart Plaza, Chicago, Ill. 60654

Focal Press. Focal Press, Inc.: refer orders to: Pitman Publishing Co., 20 East 46th St., New York, N.Y. 10017

Follett. Follett Publishing Co., 1010 West Washington Blvd., Chicago, Ill. 60607

Fortune. Time Inc., 540 North Michigan Ave., Chicago, Ill. 60611

Free Pr. Free Press. See Macmillan.

Frontier Pr. The Frontier Press Co., 815 Lafayette Bldg., Buffalo, N.Y. 14203

Funk. Funk & Wagnalls Company, Inc., 380 Madison Ave., New York, N.Y. 10017

Gale Res. Gale Research Co., 1400 Book Tower, Detroit, Mich. 48226

Gall. Gall & Inglis, Publishers, 12 Newington Rd., Edinburgh 9, Scotland

Gemological Institute of America. 11940 Van Vicente Blvd., Los Angeles, Calif. 90049

Golden Pr. Golden Press. See Western

Goodheart-Willcox. Goodheart-Willcox Co., 18250 Harwood Ave., Homewood, Ill. 60430

Govt. Print. Off. Government Printing Office, Washington, D.C. 20401

Grolier. Grolier, Inc., 575 Lexington Ave., New York, N.Y. 10022

Gründ. Dr. Med. Alois Gründ. See Boston Book and Art Shop, Inc.

Hammond. Hammond, Inc., 515 Valley St., Maplewood, N.J. 07040

Harcourt. Harcourt, Brace & World, Inc., 757 Third Ave., New York, N.Y. 10017

Harper. Harper & Row, Publishers, 49 East 33d St., New York, N.Y. 10016

Hart. Hart Publishing Co., Inc.: refer orders to: Keystone Industrial Park, Scranton, Pa. 18512

Harvard Univ. Pr. Harvard University Press, Publishing Dept., 79 Garden St., Cambridge, Mass. 02138

Hawthorn. Hawthorn Books, Inc., 70 Fifth Ave., New York, N.Y. 10011

Heath. D. C. Heath & Company, 285 Columbus Ave., Boston, Mass. 02116

Heinemann. William Heinemann, Ltd.: refer orders to: William Heinemann, Ltd., The Press at Kingswood, Tadworth, Surrey, England

Herder. B. Herder Book Co., 314 North Jefferson Ave., St. Louis, Mo. 63103

Hill & Wang. Hill & Wang, Inc., 141 Fifth Ave., New York, N.Y. 10010

Hillary House. Hillary House Publishers, Ltd., 303 Park Ave. S., New York, N.Y. 10010

Holt. Holt, Rinehart & Winston, Inc., 383 Madison Ave., New York, N.Y. 10017

Horizon. Horizon Press, Inc., 156 Fifth Ave., New York, N.Y. 10010

Houghton. Houghton Mifflin Co., 2 Park St., Boston, Mass. 02107

Index Pub. Co. Index Publishing Co., 135 William St., New York, N.Y. 10038

Industrial Press. 200 Madison Ave., New York, N.Y. 10016

Industrial Res. Ser. Industrial Research Service, Masonic Bldg., Dover, N.H. 03820

Int. City Managers. The International City Managers' Association, 1313 East 60th St., Chicago, Ill. 60637

Int. Pub. Ser. International Publications Service, 303 Park Ave. S., New York, N.Y. 10010

James F. Carr. 41 Fifth Ave., New York, N.Y. 10003

Jewish Pub. The Jewish Publication Society of America, 222 North 15th St., Philadelphia, Pa. 19102

Johnson Pub. Co. Johnson Publishing Co., Inc., Book Division, 1820 South Michigan Ave., Chicago, Ill. 60616

Johnson Publishing Co., Inc., Box 455, Loveland, Colo. 80537

Johnston. W. & A. K. Johnston & G. W. Bacon, Ltd., Edina Works, Easter Rd., Edinburgh 7, Scotland

Kenedy. P. J. Kenedy & Son, 12 Barclay St., New York, N.Y. 10007

Kenkyusha. Kenkyusha, Ltd., Publishers, 1 Fujimicho, 2-Chome, Chiyodaku, Tokyo, Japan

Klein. B. Klein & Co., 104 Fifth Ave., New York, N.Y. 10011

Knopf. Alfred A. Knopf, Inc.: refer orders to: 33 West 60th St., New York, N.Y. 10023

Kosciusko Foundation. 15 East 65th St., New York, N.Y. 10021

Ktav. Ktav Publishing House, 120 East Broadway, New York, N.Y. 10002

Lea & Febiger. 600 South Washington Sq., Philadelphia, Pa. 19106

Library of Congress. Washington, D.C. 20540

Lippincott. J. B. Lippincott Co., East Washington Sq., Philadelphia, Pa. 19105

Little. Little, Brown & Company, 34 Beacon St., Boston, Mass. 02106

Louisiana State Univ. Pr. Louisiana

State University Press, Baton Rouge, La. 70803

McGraw-Hill. McGraw-Hill Book Co., Inc., 330 West 42d St., New York, N.Y. 10036

McKay. David McKay Co., Inc., 750 Third Ave., New York, N.Y. 10017

Macmillan. The Macmillan Co., 866 Third Ave., New York, N.Y. 10022

Marquis. The A. N. Marquis Co., Inc., 200 East Ohio St., Chicago, Il. 60611

Mass. Inst. of Technology. Massachusetts Institute of Technology, Publications Office (M.I.T. Press), 77 Massachusetts Ave., Cambridge, Mass. 02139

Merck. Merck & Co., Inc., 126 East Lincoln Ave., Rahway, N.J. 07065

Meredith. Meredith Corp., 1716 Locust St., Des Moines, Ia. 50303

Merriam. G. & C. Merriam Co., 47 Federal St., Springfield, Mass. 01101

Microcard Editions, Inc. 901 26th St. N.W., Washington, D.C. 20037

Moody Press. 820 North LaSalle St., Chicago, Ill. 60610

Nat. Assn. of Social Workers. National Association of Social Workers, Inc., 2 Park Ave., New York, N.Y. 10016

Nat. Ind. Conf. Bd. National Industrial Conference Board, Inc., 845 Third Ave., New York, N.Y. 10022

Nat. Press. National Press Publications, 850 Hansen Way, Palo Alto, Calif. 94304

National Academy of Sciences—National Research Council. 2101 Constitution Ave. N.W., Washington, D.C. 20418

National Association for Mental Health, Inc. 10 Columbus Circle,

Suite 1300, New York, N.Y. 10019

National Council of the Churches of Christ in the U.S.A. Office of Publication & Distribution, 475 Riverside Dr., New York, N.Y. 10027

National Geographic Soc. National Geographic Society, 17th & M Sts. N.W., Washington, D.C. 20036

Nelson. Thomas Nelson & Sons, Copewood & Davis Sts., Camden, N.J. 08103

New Amer. Lib. New American Library of World Literature, Inc., 1301 Avenue of the Americas, New York, N.Y. 10019

New York Graphic. New York Graphic Society, Ltd., 140 Greenwich Ave., Greenwich, Conn. 06830

New York Times Co. 229 W. 43d St., New York, N.Y. 10036, Attn.: Book Editorial Dept.

New York Univ. Pr. New York University Press, Inc., 32 Washington Pl., New York, N.Y. 10003

Newspaper Enterprise Assn., Inc. 7 East 43d St., New York, N.Y. 10017

Noonday. The Noonday Press, 19 Union Sq. W., New York, N.Y. 10003

Odyssey. Odyssey Press: refer orders to: Trade Div., 850 Third Ave., New York, N.Y. 10022

Oxbridge Pub. Co. Oxbridge Publishing Co., 420 Lexington Ave., New York, N.Y. 10017

Oxford Univ. Pr. Oxford University Press: refer orders to: 1600 Pollitt Dr., Fair Lawn, N.J. 07410

Penguin. Penguin Books, Inc.: refer orders to: Houghton Mifflin Co., 2 Park St., Boston, Mass. 02107

Peter Smith. 6 Lexington Ave., Magnolia, Mass. 01930

Philip. George Philip & Son, Ltd., 98 Victoria Road, London, N.W. 10, England

Pitman. Pitman Publishing Corp., 20 East 46th St., New York, N.Y. 10017

Pocket Bks. Pocket Books, 630 Fifth Ave., New York, N.Y. 10020

Praeger. Frederick A. Praeger, Inc. 111 Fourth Ave., New York, N.Y. 10003

Prayer Bk. Pr. Prayer Book Press, Inc.: refer orders to: Taplinger Publishing Co., Inc., 29 East Tenth St., New York, N.Y. 10003

Prentice-Hall. Prentice-Hall, Inc., Englewood Cliffs, N.J. 07632

Princeton Univ. Pr. Princeton University Press, Princeton, N.J. 08540

Public Affairs Information Service. 11 West 40th St., New York, N.Y. 10018

Public Affairs Press. 419 New Jersey Ave. S.E., Washington, D.C. 20003

Putnam. G. P. Putnam's Sons, 200 Madison Ave., New York, N.Y. 10016

Quigley. Quigley Publishing Co., Inc., 1270 Sixth Ave., New York, N.Y.10020

Rand McNally. Rand McNally & Co., Box 7600, Chicago, Ill. 60680

Random House. Random House, Inc.: refer orders to: 33 West 60th St., New York, N.Y. 10023

Reinhold. Reinhold Publishing Corp., Book Div., 430 Park Ave., New York, N.Y. 10022

Richard Gordon and Associates. P.O. Box 611, Columbia, Miss. 65201

Ronald. The Ronald Press Co., 79 Madison Ave., New York, N.Y. 10016

Russell Sage. Russell Sage Foundation, 230 Park Ave., New York, N.Y. 10017

S.F. Book Imports. Box 526, San Francisco, Calif. 94101

S. G. Phillips. S. G. Phillips, Inc.: refer orders to: Hill & Wang, 141 Fifth Ave., New York, N.Y. 10010

Sales Management. 630 Third Ave., New York, N.Y. 10017

Sams. The Howard W. Sams Co., Inc. See Bobbs.

Sargent. Porter Sargent, Publisher, 11 Beacon St., Boston, Mass. 02108

Saunders. W. B. Saunders Co., West Washington Sq., Philadelphia, Pa. 19105

Scarecrow. Scarecrow Press, Inc., 52 Liberty St., Metuchen, N.J. 08840

Schirmer. G. Schirmer, Inc., 609 Fifth Ave., New York, N.Y. 10017

Schocken. Schocken Books, Inc., 67 Park Ave., New York, N.Y. 10016

Schoenhof. Schoenhof's Foreign Books, Inc., 1280 Massachusetts Ave., Cambridge, Mass. 02138

Scott. Scott, Foresman & Co., 1900 East Lake Ave., Glenview, Ill. 60025

Scott Publications, Inc.: refer orders to: M. Meghrig & Sons, 239 Park Ave. S., New York, N.Y. 10003

Scribner. Charles Scribner's Sons, 597 Fifth Ave., New York, N.Y. 10017

Shoe String. The Shoe String Press, Inc., 60 Connolly Pkwy., Hamden, Conn. 06514

Simon & Schuster. Simon & Schuster, Inc.: refer orders to: 1 West 39th St., New York, N.Y. 10018

South-Western. South-Western Publishing Co., 5101 Madison Rd., Cincinnati, O. 45227

Special Libraries Assn. 31 East Tenth St., New York, N.Y. 10003

Springer Pub. Springer Publishing Co., Inc., 200 Park Ave. S., New York, N.Y. 10003

St. Martin's. St. Martin's Press, Inc., 175 Fifth Ave., New York, N.Y. 10010

Stackpole. Stackpole Books, Cameron & Kelker Sts., Harrisburg, Pa. 17105

Taplinger. Taplinger Publishing Co., Inc., 29 East Tenth St., New York, N.Y. 10003

Thomas Pub. Thomas Publishing Co., 461 Eighth Ave., New York, N.Y. 10001

Transatlantic Arts. Transatlantic Arts, Inc.: refer orders to: 105 Blue Spruce Rd., Levittown, N.Y. 11756

Tudor. Tudor Publishing Co., 221 Park Ave. S., New York, N.Y. 10003

Tuttle, Charles E. Tuttle Co., Inc., 28 South Main St., Rutland, Vt. 05701

U.N. Publications. United Nations Publications. Sales Section. United Nations, Office of Public Information, Room 1059, New York, N.Y. 10017

UNESCO. UNESCO Publications Center, 317 East 34th St., New York, N.Y. 10016

Ungar. Frederick Ungar Publishing Co., 250 Park Ave. S., New York, N.Y. 10003

Univ. of California Pr. University of California Press: refer orders to: 223 Fulton St., Berkeley, Calif. 94720

Univ. of Chicago Pr. University of Chicago Press, 5750 Ellis Ave., Chicago, Ill. 60637

Univ. of Illinois Pr. University of Illinois Press, Urbana, Ill. 61801

Univ. of Michigan Pr. University of Michigan Press, 615 East University Ave., Ann Arbor, Mich. 48106

Univ. of Minnesota Pr. University of Minnesota Press, 2037 University Ave. S.E., Minneapolis, Minn. 55455

Univ. of Toronto Pr. University of Toronto Press, Front Campus, Toronto 5, Ont., Canada

Van Nostrand. D. Van Nostrand Co., Inc., 120 Alexander St., Princeton, N.J. 08540

Viking. The Viking Press, Inc., 625 Madison Ave., New York, N.Y. 10022

Vintage. Vintage Books: refer orders to: Random House, Inc., 33 West 60th St., New York, N.Y. 10023

W. C. Brown. William C. Brown Co., 135 South Locust St., Dubuque, Ia. 52001

Warne. Frederick Warne & Co., Inc., 101 Fifth Ave., New York, N.Y. 10003

Washburn. Ives Washburn, Inc. *See* McKay.

Washington Square. Washington Square Press: refer orders to: Simon & Schuster, Inc., 1 West 39th St., New York, N.Y. 10018

Wayne State Univ. Pr. Wayne State University Press, 5980 Cass St., Detroit, Mich. 48202

Western. Western Publishing Co., 850 Third Ave., New York, N.Y. 10022

Westminster. The Westminster Press, Witherspoon Bldg., Walnut & Juniper Sts., Philadelphia, Pa. 19107

Whitaker. Joseph Whitaker & Sons, Ltd., 13 Bedford Sq., London W.C.1, England

Whitman. Whitman Publishing Co., 1220 Mound Ave., Racine, Wis. 53404

Wiley, John Wiley & Sons, Inc., 605 Third Ave., New York, N.Y. 10016

Williams & Wilkins. The Williams & Wilkins Co., 428 East Preston St., Baltimore, Md. 21202

Wilson. H. W. Wilson Co., 950 University Ave., Bronx, N.Y. 10452

World Trade. World Trade Academy Press, Inc.: refer orders to: Regents Publishing Co., 200 Park Ave. S., New York, N.Y. 10003

Writer. The Writer, Inc., 8 Arlington St., Boston, Mass. 02116

Writer's Digest. 22 East Twelfth St., Cincinnati, O. 45210

Yale Univ. Pr. Yale University Press: refer orders to: 149 York St., New Haven, Conn. 06511

Year. Year, Inc., 20 West 45th St., New York, N.Y. 10036

Index

Numbers listed refer to entries and not to pages. An "n" after a number indicates that the work is mentioned in the annotation.

Book reviews, 11, 14, 17–18

Book trade *see* Printing and publishing

Booklist and Subscription books bulletin, 11

Books in print, 2

Botkin, B. A. Treasury of American folklore, 93

Boutell, C. Boutell's Heraldry, 627

Brady, G. S. Materials handbook, 288

Brandon, M. M., and Stetka, F. NFPA handbook of the National electrical code, 286

Breasted, J. H. Conquest of civilization, 544

Brewer, E. C. Dictionary of phrase and fable, 474

Bridgwater, W., and Kurtz, S., eds. Columbia encyclopedia, 51

Briggs, M. S. Everyman's concise encyclopedia of architecture, 329

Britannica book of the year, 48

British authors before 1800, S. J. Kunitz and H. Haycraft, eds., 600

British authors of the 19th century, S. J. Kunitz and H. Haycraft, eds., 601

Brockhaus illustrated German-English, English-German dictionary, 434

Brooke-Little, J. P., and Scott-Giles, C. W. Boutell's Heraldry, 627

Brown, G. W., Trudel, M., and Vachon, A., eds. Dictionary of Canadian biography, 583

Brown, R. C., and Ploski, H. A. Negro almanac, 163

Buddhism *see* Religion

Buddhism in translations, H. C. Warren, ed. and tr., 86

Budget in brief, U.S. Bureau of the Budget, 105

Bulas, K., Thomas, L. L., and Whitfield, F. J. Kosciusko Foundation dictionary: English-Polish, Polish-English, 445

Bulfinch, T. Bulfinch's Mythology, 94

Bulletin, Public Affairs Information Service, 22

Burke, W. J., and Howe, W. D. American authors and books, 475

Burt, W. H., and Grossenheider, R. P. Field guide to the mammals, 272

Business, 101–3, 107–25, 127–45, 147–51

Business management, 123, 130, 140, 145, 147

Business periodicals index, 103, 232n

Buss, C. A. Asia in the modern world, 571

Butler, A. Lives of the saints, 615

Callaham, L. I. Russian-English chemical and polytechnical dictionary, 253

Cambridge bibliography of English literature. F. W. Bateson, ed., 458

Cambridge history of English literature. A. W. Ward and A. R. Waller, eds., 464

Cambridge Italian dictionary, B. Reynolds, ed., 440

Campbell, G., and Evans, I. O. Book of flags, 628

Campbell, O. J., and Quinn, E. G., eds. Reader's encyclopedia of Shakespeare, 490

Campbell, R. J., and Hinsie, L. E. Psychiatric dictionary, 303

Canada, 165, 577, 583

Canadian almanac and directory, 165

Career and vocational school guide, C. E. Lovejoy, 221

Carruth, G. Encyclopedia of American facts and dates, 533

Cartter, A. M., ed. American universities and colleges, 211; Assessment of quality in graduate education, 227

Cary, M., ed. Oxford classical dictionary, 507

Cases in constitutional law, R. E. Cushman and R. F. Cushman, 192

Cass, J., and Birnbaum, M. Comparative guide to American colleges, 213

Cassell's Encyclopedia of world literature, S. H. Steinberg, ed., 469

Cassell's New Latin dictionary; Latin-English, English-Latin, 443

Cassell's Spanish-English, English-Spanish dictionary, 453

Catalog of reprints in series, R. M. Orton, 7

Catalogue of color reproductions, 1860–1965, UNESCO, 367

Catalogue of color reproductions of paintings prior to 1860, UNESCO, 366

Catalogue of the world's most popular coins, F. Reinfeld, 338

Catholic dictionary, D. Attwater, ed., 55

Catholic encyclopedia, C. G. Herbermann, 63

Cazamian, L. F. History of French literature, 497

Census, United States, 172–75

Census of population, U.S. Bureau of the Census, 172

Ceramics, 304–42

Chaffers, W. Marks and monograms on European and Oriental pottery and porcelain, 340

Challinor, J. Dictionary of geology, 260

Chandler, R. E., and Schwartz, K. New history of Spanish literature, 503

Chemical publications, M. G. Mellon, 258

Chemistry, 253–55, 257–59

Cheney, S. New world history of art, 322

Child care, 300

Chinese-English dictionary (Rev. American ed.), R. H. Mathéws, 428

Chinese-English dictionary (Rev. English index), R. H. Mathews, 429

Chronology, 205–6, 533, 539, 545

Chu, Hung-fu. How to know the immature insects, 273

Church, J. M., and Simonds, H. R. Concise guide to plastics, 313

Citizen's band radio handbook, D. E. Hicks, 284

Civil War dictionary, M. M. Boatner, 531

Clans, septs, and regiments of the Scottish highlands, F. Adams, 626

Clark, G. L., and Hawley, G. G., eds. Encyclopedia of chemistry, 254

Clark, R. L., and Cumley, R. W., eds. Book of health, 295

Classic myths in English literature and in art, C. M. Gayley, 95

Classical antiquities, 507–8, 523

Classical literature, 505–12

Classical myths in English literature, D. S. Norton and P. Rushton, 96

Cleaning and dyeing, 310

Cochran, T. C., and Andrews, W., eds. Concise dictionary of American history, 535

Colby, V., and Kunitz, S. J., eds. European authors, 1000–1900, 605; Twentieth century authors, 1st supplement, 604

Coleman, H., and Shaw, M. F. National anthems of the world, 386

Collector's glossary of antiques and fine arts, J. R. Bernasconi, 345

College Entrance Examination Board. College handbook, 214

College guide, C. E. Lovejoy, 223

College handbook, College Entrance Examination Board, 214

College placement directory, O. T. Zimmerman and M. Zimmerman, 119

Jones and P. B. Schubert, eds., 291

England, 560-61

English, H. B., and English, A. C. Comprehensive dictionary of psychological and psychoanalytical terms, 99

English language, 399-427

English literature, 95-96, 457-58, 464-65, 468, 470, 477, 488-94

English-Russian dictionary, V. K. Müller, comp., 450

Ergang, R. R. Europe from the Renaissance to Waterloo, 553; Europe in our time, 555; Europe since Waterloo, 554

Essay and general literature index, 460

Ethridge, J. M., Thomas, R. C., and Ruffner, F. G., eds. Acronyms and initialisms dictionary, 407

Etiquette, 203-4

Etiquette, E. P. Post, 203

Etymological dictionary of the English language, W. W. Skeat, 412

Europe, 207, 543, 551-59; *see also* by country in Europe, e.g., France

Europe from the Renaissance to Waterloo, R. R. Ergang, 553

Europe in our time, R. R. Ergang, 555

Europe since Waterloo, R. R. Ergang, 554

European authors, 1000-1900, S. J. Kunitz and V. Colby, eds., 605

Evans, B., and Evans, C. Dictionary of contemporary American usage, 424

Evans, I. O., and Campbell, G. Book of flags, 628

Evans, M. Costume through the ages, 370

Everyman's concise encyclopedia of architecture, M. S. Briggs, 329

Everyman's concise encyclopedia of Russia, S. Utechin, 567

Everyman's dictionary of non-classical mythology, E. Sykes, comp., 92

Everyman's United Nations, 201

Ewen, D. Composers of yesterday, 609n; Encyclopedia of the opera, 376; Great composers, 609; Living musicians, 610; New book of modern composers, 611; Popular American composers from Revolutionary times to the present, 612; World of great composers from Palestrina to Debussy, 611n, 613

Exhaustive concordance of the Bible, J. Strong, 81

Expenditure patterns of the American family, National Industrial Conference Board, 144

Exporters' encyclopaedia, L. Kerr, ed., 122

Factbook on man, L. I. Dublin, 299

Facts about the Presidents, J. N. Kane, 587

Fairholt, F. W. Dictionary of terms in art, 316n

Fairy tales, 87

Falls, C. Great war, 1914-1918, 556

Familiar quotations, J. Bartlett, 483

Famous first facts, J. N. Kane, 538

Fannie Farmer cook book, F. M. Farmer, 306, 308n

Farmer, F. M. Fannie Farmer cook book, 306

Fashion dictionary, M. B. Picken, 373

Feather, L. G. Encyclopedia of jazz, 377; Encyclopedia of jazz in the sixties, 377a

Feder, L. Crowell's Handbook of classical literature, 505

Federal career directory, U.S. Civil Service Commission, 229

Feingold, S. N. Scholarships, fellowships, and loans, 228

Fellowships and scholarships, 222, 225, 228

Festivals of Western Europe, D. G. Spicer, 207

Fiction, 15, 459, 476, 479

Fiction catalog, 15